MW01235719

A Journey of Faith, Family and Future

Bishop of Dorsetshire

A JOURNEY OF FAITH, FAMILY AND FUTURE:

FIVE GENERATIONS OF THE

BISHOP FAMILY

Kay Shepard, Bobby
Bishop and Billy Bishop

A Journey of Faith, Family and Future:
Five Generations of the Bishop Family

Bilbo Books Publishing
www.BilboBooks.com

ISBN- 978-0-9981627-3-7
ISBN- 0-9981627-3-6

Printed in the United States of America

Bilbo Books Publishing
ATHENS, GEORGIA

Contents

Harrell and Kathleen Bishop

PROLOGUE

Come take a journey with us. A journey that spans over 100 years. A journey which begins in a time when God, family and hard work were the very essence of American life. For us, the Bishop family, this journey begins in the early nineteen hundreds in Georgia, travels south to Florida, turns around and heads back to Georgia, then back to Florida again, and finally ends up back here in Georgia in the 21st century at a time when it seems as if the values we hold dear are under attack. Taking this journey with us, the children of Harrell and Kathleen Bishop, will give you a glimpse into the past, present and the future legacy of our family.

Picture three siblings sitting around a small dining table in a cozy cottage, a white, one-story guest cottage, the centerpiece of a 410-acre farm in northeast Georgia. The land was once almost completely rural, peach trees, crop rows and Farm Bureau Saturday nights. Nowadays, it's a little more developed. It still retains the flavor of a simpler time, but with quick access to tanning beds, Middle-Eastern restaurants, and other amenities of "civilization" unheard of in previous generations.

At this round, oak, slightly-worn, well-loved table sit three siblings:

Kay---(the responsible older sister who strives to keep her siblings on track)

Bobby---(the jovial, but solid, rock of the family, creating hay sculptures for each season and managing family business)

Billy---(the rebellious and witty one, forever thinking of ways to slightly disrupt the equilibrium and entertain those around him, also the one who does the physical labor)

Billy---...and what was that, the third time I was hit by a car?

Kay---The second.

Billy (voice slightly raised)---No, the second time was when I was dragged down the beach by that car.

Bobby---How have you managed to survive this long?

Billy---Sheer will power.

Kay---(after a brief, reflective pause)---Not to get too deep, but we've done a lot over the years.

Bobby---True. We've got a heck'uva story to tell.

Billy---Like that time we started that snowball fight with those UGA frat boys?

Bobby---Well yeah, but not just the messes you've gotten us into over the years, Billy.

Billy---Hey, those were some pretty creative messes.

Kay---Admittedly, but Bobby's right. We've got a story to tell.

Bobby---To pass on.

Billy---You're just saying that 'cause you're a teacher.

Kay---And yet I'm still not allowed to paddle you.

Bobby---Like your high school history teacher did that time he caught you chewing gum in class.

Billy---Five licks with a big ole' paddle.

Bobby---They didn't mess around in those days, did they?

Billy---And the guy was a Navy veteran, too. Y'all are right, though. We do have a pretty good story to tell.

Bobby---How else are our grandkids going to learn their family history and adopt our values? Hard work and fearing God may not be the most popular ideas these days, but they still matter to us.

Billy---And the time I got those screw worms.

Kay---Oh, my Lord, I can still smell those disgusting things. Maybe we shouldn't include stuff like that.

Billy---Oh, come on. We've got to have things like that. That's the good stuff!

Bobby---(to Kay) I hate to say it, but Billy's right.

Kay---Fine. But if we're going to use things like that then it's got to show our Christian values, too. It's got to talk about pride, patriotism, family, love, the big, important things.

Billy---And a complete listing of all of my many impressive injuries.

Kay---All of your injuries? All of them? If we put all of them in there the book will be 1000 pages.

Bobby---Surely we can strike the right balance. And I want to people to know how we helped the bank, how we made the first public swimming pool in the county, and how we even let the D.O.T. take our land for the highway.

Kay---As if we had a choice.

Billy---Eminent domain? They should call it what it is, highway robbery.

Kay---If we include our parents' story, we might even have enough for a decent book.

Bobby---Yeah, Mother and Daddy went through some tough times and came out the other side, didn't they?

FAST FORWARD FIVE MINUTES INTO THE FUTURE (the three talking about what they would include in a family memoir)

Billy---Did you get the belt? (Billy stands and dramatically whips off his belt to demonstrate the signature sound of their father when he was angry.) Come on, tell us. Did Daddy whoop you for that one?

Bobby---Did he whoop me for it? Are you kidding? When I told him "I quit" he hit me with a dern' vacuum hose.

Billy---Ohh, you got the hose?

Kay---I bet you learned that lesson. What about all the little life lessons from working the dairies in Daytona?

Bobby---Holly Hill.

Kay---Well, I know it was Holly Hill, Bobby. I was there, too, but everybody knows about Daytona. Nobody's ever heard of Holly Hill.

Billy---They'll know about it once we write the book.

Bobby---If we're going to do this, to write this book, we're going to have to do it right, you know?

Kay---Of course. That goes without saying, Bobby. We wouldn't be Harrell Bishop's kids if we did a half-hearted job.

Bobby---Yeah, Daddy sure stressed that one, the personal satisfaction of doing a job and doing it well.

Billy---We're all retired now. We've got time. Let's do this…but I'm definitely putting the screw worms in there.

(Kay shakes her head, lovingly, in a gesture honed over decades as the older sister, while simultaneously beginning to plan how to turn this rambling conversation into a readable, interesting, morally-relevant family memoir)

INTRODUCTION

Like our family itself and almost everything we have ever done, the writing of this book was a truly collaborative effort. Being raised on a dairy farm, we know how to do chores, but we still divide the labor in order to get it all done before supper time. Kay, Bobby and Billy's voices are all heard throughout the story. Even our dearly departed brother, Radford, lends his voice to the story, through his children, and through our cherished memories. Sometimes, in order to provide an objective outsider perspective, one of our publishers takes the reins. Although we are siblings, raised under the same roof, by the same parents, and taught the same moral lessons, we're still different people with different points of view. Collectively and individually, we've been blessed with some of the best gifts a loving God can bestow on anyone: faith, family, and fertile land.

We, Kay Bishop Shepard, H. Radford Bishop, Billy Bishop and Bobby Bishop are a group of siblings who have accepted and practiced the values of our parents with religious devotion. We have taken in trust 410 acres of land our father acquired in Watkinsville, and developed virtually every square inch of it in a way that will benefit others and enhance the community as a whole.

It is not only our home, but includes a residential subdivision, a lake, a bank, an amphitheater, and a college, as well as a working cattle operation spanning the breadth of the land.

A cottage sits in the middle of it all, a cottage with a spectacular panoramic view of acres of pastures stretching back into the woods. The sight reminds the viewer of that scene from "Gone with the Wind" where Gerald O'Hara says, "The land is the only thing that matters, the land is the only thing that lasts." As we gaze out the sliding glass back doors of the cottage and let our

minds wander back to a simpler time, we are reminded that on the third day God created the land, and on the sixth day He created the living creatures that move along that ground. Glancing out our back door reminds us that land is opportunity, the opportunity to use this sacred trust in a positive and productive way, a way that enhances the lives of everyone around us.

This sacred trust, diligently passed onto us by our parents, is the result of an abiding faith in God and the goals we were taught to pursue without blinders. We learned that work feeds the soul. We learned that life is about more than the pursuit of money. It's about pride. It's about purpose. It's about fulfillment.

It's easy to see the fruits of your labors on a farm, but it's possible to see the fruits in other jobs, other life paths, as well. Filling milk jars is conveniently measurable, but other jobs are measurable, too. Filling out insurance forms or selling houses are measurable.

Putting your feet up at the end of a long day, looking back at the result of your labors and taking pride in what you have accomplished is a daily goal.

This is the Bishop story, a family memoir that has lessons for us all.

The Bishops have been dairy farmers and beef cattlemen for three generations. It's a large part of who we are. If you want to trace the reason for this back to its origin, we'd have to credit the *boll weevil*. Everyone in our generation knows what a boll weevil is. We all grew up hearing the horror stories. Our parents and grandparents knew the boll weevil all too intimately. Anthonomus grandis, more commonly called the boll weevil, was the scourge of the South, the destroyer of cotton plantations, the impetus that sent thousands of farming families out of their ancestral homes and onto the great American road, in search of a new dream.

The quest was motivated by financial desperation. Bobby likes to say, "If you want to trace somebody's history, check their check book." This saying certainly applied to our family. It was the dwindling check book balances in Georgia that put our grandparents on the road. In the case of the Bishop and Summerlin families, that road took them to Daytona Beach, Florida, in the middle of a Florida Boom Era, the roaring 1920's.

These days, Daytona is best known as a tourist town, a NASCAR hub, and a vacation spot for families and rowdy college kids on Spring Break. It was a vacation spot in our day, too, but it was also home. We ran along the beach on Sunday afternoons. We frolicked in the ocean. We listened with rapt attention to the radio serials of the 1950's, vicariously enjoying the audio adventures of the Green Hornet. Thanks to our father's love of boxing, we all remember listening to the Friday Night Fights, thrilled by the action racing through our father's old RCA radio. But, mainly, we worked. Running a dairy farm takes a lot of work. It's a never-ending, 24/7, 365 days-a-year task, a rigid world with un-breakable rules that must be obeyed or the whole structure comes crashing down upon you. That's the world we were born into. That is our legacy.

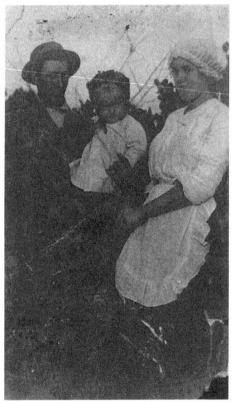

Thad and Mozelle with Harrel

CHAPTER ONE

STARVING IN GEORGIA

Both of our sets of grandparents migrated to Florida at approximately the same time: Eva and Lemuel Summerlin ("Eva" and "Lem" to us), and Mozelle and Thaddaeus Bishop ("Big Momma" and "Thad"). Big Momma was a Lovern before she married into the Bishop family. She was the only Lovern to leave Georgia, shoving off from her country origins for a life in the city.

After two grueling days of travel, Mozelle Bishop, our paternal grandmother, along with Harrell, her intrepid twelve-year-old explorer son (who would later become our father), and his two sisters, Sarah and Doris, arrived in Port Orange, Florida from The Agnes Scott Hotel in Bostwick, Georgia, near the Lovern family home at High Shoals, on our nation's one-hundred-and-fiftieth birthday, July 4, 1926. Our father, despite his tender age, drove most of the way himself in the family's shiny, new 1926 Ford Touring (which cost a whopping $355, brand new, a tidy sum nearly a century ago). Mozelle, "Big Momma" to us, with her three young children in tow, was racing to meet her husband, Thaddaeus, who had departed from Atlanta, Georgia, to find work in the sunny land of orange groves and sandy beaches. Leaving for greener pastures, our grandparents must have averaged about 200 miles/day to reach Port Orange, a small town just south of

Daytona Beach in just two days. That's a lot of ground to cover in a small amount of time, especially when you consider the poor road conditions nearly a century ago and the top speed of the Ford Touring.

It was the plague of the boll weevil that drove them farther south, along with so many other desperate families. At the time, Sarah was eight and Doris was just six-years-old. Sadly, both of Daddy's younger sisters passed away before they could turn twenty-five. Life was tough back then.

As a boy, Daddy managed to enjoy life while honing his work ethic. It's not an easy dual-lesson to pull off, but Harrell Bishop was never one to choose a path because it looked easy. His childhood jobs ranged from Western Union telegraph deliverer (being an angel of good news) to exercising horses by riding them up and down the famed sands of Daytona Beach (the coolest, most cowboyesque job ever for a child in coastal Florida). He also shopped for the family's groceries, carrying them home on his bicycle, and running errands for his father's feed and livestock customers. Life was exciting and fun in the "Sunshine State."

In the early 1930's Thad and Mozelle opened a dairy at 11th Street in Holly Hill, Florida, called the Bishop Dairy. Daddy had worked with his father at the Bishop Dairy as a young man. He hadn't planned on making dairy farming his livelihood, but life throws us all a few curveballs. In the 1930's, in the heart of America's Great Depression, he joined his father in the dairy business.

Daddy began his chapter of the family dairy farming story

in the late 1940's with just one cow. If it wasn't for that cow, we wouldn't be here today. He sold fresh milk to his neighbors to earn extra money, unaware that he was starting the family business. If he'd known, he could have bronzed that cow and we could place her out in front of the family farm to welcome our visitors. Barbershops and restaurants frame the first dollar they earned, and that's not nearly as interesting as a bronzed cow.

The earliest records find our maternal grandparents, Eva and Lem Summerlin, running a hotel in Georgia around 1900, before they migrated south to Florida. The Summerlins had run the Summerlin Hotel in Willacoochee, Georgia, a railroad town linking Albany to the coastal town of Brunswick, since 1895. They kept their doors open until the rash of massive farm failures made it impossible for them to earn a living. Eva and Lem fol-

Thad, Mozelle, Harrell and Sarah

lowed closely on the heels of their son, Fred Summerlin, who had left Willacoochee earlier and found mill work in Florida, making quality millwork for new construction, mainly for dormitories. They later changed the name of their company to The Summerlin Brothers Mill Works.

Willacoochee wasn't as much of a physical part of our collective childhood as it had been for Eva and Lem, but we heard plenty of stories of life below the Georgia Gnat Line, the constant fight against the insects and the overpowering humidity, the cotton life, and fishing the flooded ditches. What a great name for a town.

Eva and Lem were an impressive couple and accomplished individuals. Eva had studied "Voice" at Breneau College. As hard as it may be to believe, coming from the perspective of a time where women are free to do whatever men can, that wasn't

Summerlin Hotel in Willacoochee, GA

the way it was in our grandparents' day. It was rare for women to attend college in those days. Most women were married and working on their second child by age eighteen back in the late nineteenth century, but Eva was a strong and determined woman as well as a classically-trained singer. She had grown up following her father on a local preaching circuit, going town to town, revival to revival. He would preach and she would sing the

Eva West Summerlin

hymns, leading to her pursuit of a musical life. Lem was always an entrepreneur at heart. We remember him as he was when we were children, older, in his white pants and white shoes, but, from the family stories we grew up on, we learned that Lem was one of those American men who always looked for new and inventive ways to make money. They ran The Prospect Inn, a "Tourist Home," or boarding house, on Ridgewood Avenue in Daytona Beach, Florida, a guest home which still stands today. That hard-charging, slavishly-working, never-complacent, entrepreneurial spirit has survived the changes in American society, the rise of the Information Age, and the ever-shifting winds of social, political, and financial change that have always been a part of the American story.

Change is definitely a large part of the Bishop Family story. We weather change, but we never forget who we are. Thanks to our parents, their parents, and their parents before them, we've learned some valuable lessons, lessons that we want to pass down to you, which you can then impart to your children, and so forth. Read closely. This is our story, which means that it's your story, too.

Mother's family at Prospect Inn

Prospect Inn, Daytona Beach

CHAPTER TWO

THE ENCHANTING CITY

Daytona Beach, The Enchanting City, grew as the Florida boom of the early 20th century drew Americans from all over the country to Florida. That part of the state was first claimed by The United States by Andrew Jackson in 1814, a result of winning The Seminole Wars against the fearsome and tenacious Indian tribe. The town itself was named for a Mister Day, who settled the area from the ocean inland, as there were no roads connecting it to the rest of the country at the time. Port Orange was the more agricultural area near the beach town, full of orange groves and cattle grazing land. Our father had one foot in each of those worlds, both a "city life" and a "country life."

We grew up with our lives entangled in both of those worlds. Yes, we were dairymen, but we were meeting people from all over the country and the world. Yes, we attended a cosmopolitan church with traveling congregants from exotic places, but we still got up at the crack of dawn to work the farm. It's not the easiest upbringing to describe in a few tight, concise phrases, but

Daddy's H.S. Football team

Mother's Basketball Team

Kathleen and friends Daytona Beach

that's part of why we had to write a book about it.

Momma and Daddy both graduated from Mainland High School in 1933, in the heart of The Great Depression. They were both athletes. Momma played basketball and Daddy was a star football player. Their high school, named Mainland, in downtown Daytona, was a small city school, where everybody knew everybody, but the two of them truly bonded in Study Hall. Study Hall is no longer a standard part of the American high school experience, but in the 1920's and 30's students had a designated hour period once a day to do their class work and study in silence. Our parents' budding love was too powerful for the rules of Study Hall. They wound up spending most of the hour passing love notes to each other and planning what they would do when they graduated, got married and started a life together. They both worked in their family businesses. Daddy worked with his father at the dairy. Momma waited tables at The Prospect Inn, a tourist home that her parents owned on Ridgewood Avenue, on the famed US 1, in Daytona Beach.

Wedding Sept. 6, 1935

Momma attended The Florida State College for Women, while Daddy pursued his football dream. He was a good fullback. Reversing the family trend, Harrell Bishop went north, from Florida to Athens, Georgia in the fall of 1933, in order to play football for The University of Georgia. The legendary UGA coach, Wally Butts, had just come to Athens from GMC (Georgia Military College), bringing his star fullback, Bill Hartman, with him. Daddy was good. Bill Hartman was really good. Daddy told us about Bill's tree-trunk-sized legs and how tough he was to bring down. Realizing that he wasn't going to get to play, Daddy transferred to Stetson College in Deland, Florida (just 20 miles from Daytona) after just one month at UGA.

Our parents were married on September 6, 1935, on Daddy's 21st birthday. Mother was also just twenty-one years old, and three months older than Daddy. They honeymooned at Tallulah Gorge, Georgia. Their fond memories of the beauty and tranquility of the northeast Georgia region around the Gorge never left their minds.

As best as we can determine, Bishop Dairy on 11th Street was started by our grandfather Thad around 1930. He had been a Pillsbury feed salesman in Atlanta, and later in Port Orange. How he came by the 50 acres or so on 11th Street is still unknown. But he started the dairy there when Daddy was still in high school. In 1935 when Mother and Daddy married, Thad offered Daddy partnership in the dairy. Daddy took the offer. We are not sure how many cows were being milked at the time, but there were about 24 milking stalls in the dairy barn. The milking machines were moved from cow to cow. Each machine would hold the milk in a 4-gallon container which hung from a belt which straddled the cows between the front and back legs. This was a labor-intensive operation. Each machine had to be unbuckled and emptied into a 10-gallon can after each cow's milking. Once the 10-gallon can was full it was then moved into the walk-in cooler in the processing room. After the cows were milked, the milk was dumped from the 10-gallon can to the 100-gallon pasteurizer tank for cooking. It was cooked at about 115 degrees Fahrenheit for several hours to kill all of the bacteria. Once it was cooled it was poured into different sized glass bottles, ½ pint for school kids, quart size for grocery stores and ½ gallon containers for homes and tourist operations/restaurant businesses.

Think about this schedule:

About 2:30 A.M. milk the cows, maybe 50 of them. Put the milking machine on each cow, dump the 20 lbs. of milk into 10-gallon milk cans 50 times, move the 10-gallon cans to the cooler, feed the cows and clean the milking barn, all to be completed by 7-8 A.M.

Then pour the 20 10-gallon cans into the pasteurizer and be sure the steam boiler produces the correct temperature, enough, but not too hot, scorching the milk.

When the milk was cooking, it was time to clean yesterday's milk bottles. We did it by hand for some, but again the steam boiler produces the clean disinfectant wash (There was a 3-stage bottle washing machine to make this process less labor-intensive) water, then rinse and dry the bottles.

The next step was to cool the pasteurized milk down over a refrigerated stainless steel cooling board into each size milk bottle. Arduous to say the least! Once the bottles were capped they were loaded into carrying crates to fit each size bottle. All went back into the cooler for delivery the next morning.

Oh, wait a minute! The cows had to be milked again that same day at 2:30 P.M.! Same routine, same 50 cows, feed, milk, same 10-gallon cans, same clean up. You can see how strenuous, grueling and physically-demanding the dairy business can be, especially if you are milking cows, processing the milk and then delivering it to your customers.

Thad and his son Harrell must have been a great team. Working side-by-side, lending each other a hand when needed. What a team!

But life has its setbacks.

Then 1941 happened. Doris died. One month later Thad died. Six months later WWII began for America with the bombing of Pearl Harbor on December 7, 1941.

After his father, Thad Bishop's, untimely death in May of 1941, the attack on Pearl Harbor, closely followed by Doris' tragic demise that same year, the Bishops entered a crisis mode the likes of which most families can barely imagine. With no other option available to him, Daddy was forced to take on the full responsibility of the family dairy. Though it was not what he had planned, Harrell Bishop proudly took up the mantel of supporting his family, including the family of his mother, and Sarah, a single parent with two small children of her own. That's a massive amount of responsibility for one man...but Daddy rose to challenge.

Daddy worked in an "Essential Services" industry, so he didn't get drafted into World War II. Farmers, metal workers, and clothing manufacturers, among others, were needed stateside to provide the food, weapons and clothing for our boys overseas. Even in Florida, though, the war affected us. Black tar washed up on the beach. Observation towers were erected on the shore to look for German U-Boats. We all had to ration. We even had to put tape over the top half of our car headlights, so they wouldn't inadvertently shine upward and disrupt pilots flying overhead.

Big Momma and Sarah needed someone to keep the family business going. Harrell stepped up! All through the war years,

Radford, Billy, Bobby First Baptist Church Daytona

mother and children Daytona st. 1947

Daddy kept it together. Dairy helpers in Florida come and go just about as often as the new moon came around. Somehow, he was able to keep that schedule going like clockwork. Of course, his own family was growing. Kay was born in 1936, Radford in 1940, Billy in 1945, and Bobby in 1946.

Another untimely event happened in 1946. Sarah's death left two small children: Barbara at 6-years-old and Doris at just age 1. So, Big Momma raised her two granddaughters for the next 20 years.

Sometime around 1950, Big Momma sold the Bishop Dairy business and built the Siesta Motel on North Atlantic Avenue, on the beach side. She remained there with Doris until her death in 1963.

Big Momma sold the dairy business to a Jewish family, who kept the Bishop Dairy name. She retained ownership of the land and barns, and rented it to the new owners. The new owners wound up selling the business sometime around 1955.

Part of the Bishop family success is that we've always been scrappy. We were born into it. Daddy was the biggest fight fan ever. He admired Jack Dempsey. He and Momma kept scrapbooks of athletes of their era. And, Lord knows, we never missed a Friday Night Fight, sponsored by Gillette, on the radio. Those radio broadcasts are some of our earliest memories. When they'd play the national anthem before the bout, Kay would stand up and put her hand over her heart. Between the rounds, Billy and Bobby would box. There was never a TKO, but there were plenty of bruises. Those were good times.

Many of our earliest memories of the house at 230 Daytona Street are on display in pictures which record the Christmas at Mary Ruth and Reno Fenders' house or in those at Virginia and Combs Young's house with the rest of the Summerlin branch of the family. There are so many childhood remembrances which should be documented, but some of the highlights around that time include: riding bikes to North Ridgewood Elementary School, digging tunnels in the backyard, finding Easter Eggs hidden in the bamboo hedges, going to Sunday school at the Loomis Building and being baptized in the old First Baptist Church sanctuary. All was good and life was family.

Christmas at Fenders 1950's

CHAPTER THREE

THE DAIRY YEARS

The regiment never changes. You wake up every day at 2 A.M. You work until 7 A.M. Then you eat and go to sleep for a few hours and wake up again around 2 P.M. and work until nightfall. Bovines aren't looking for variety in their lives. They do, however, absolutely have to be milked twice a day at the same times in order to optimize the benefits of the God-given phenomenon of turning nutritious grasses into cow's milk. Dairymen must milk their cows at the same times every day or else their whole operation will fall apart fast. You know who you are every day on a dairy. Who you are depends on where you work in the operation.

Then, around 1950 Daddy started his own dairy on 25 acres, called the Holly Hill Dairy Farm. He changed the operation from a "delivery direct to the customer" business to a "come to the dairy" approach, more commonly then called a "Cash-N-Carry" business model. He also modernized the milking plan from the old station-style to a 3-cow parlor- style. The cows came into the milking stalls 3 at a time. The stalls were elevated 2&½ feet above the floor. Also the milk went directly from the milking machines, via pipe, to a 1000-gallon stainless steel, refrigerated holding

Gurnesey cows

Holly Hill Dairy 1950's

tank 15 feet away. The milk never saw the light of day. It was all contained within a special piping and storage tank system. It was cleaner, safer, and more efficient. Now one man could milk 100 cows in the same time it had previously taken two men to milk 50 using the old station-style system employed at the 11th Street Dairy.

In 1953, the family moved from Daytona Street to 421 Flo-mich. The residence was across the street from the dairy. Daddy brought in the newest machines and expanded the product lines. The products increased from only pasteurized milk to homoge-nized milk (breaking up the butter fat into small pieces so that the butter fat did not float to the top of the bottle). We added entirely new products: chocolate, butter and even eggnog at Christmas time. Mother joined in the family work force, running the sales window for the "drive up customers." Bear in mind that even the idea of a "drive up window" was a relatively new approach to retail sales in 1950.

As if that weren't enough innovation, Mother also brought in the newest Bishop family product line, ice cream. She created flavors: banana, butter pecan, French vanilla, chocolate chip and tangerine sherbet (to name just a few). There were around 20 fla-vors in all. The local kids sure did love her ice cream. Even today we continue to hear stories, fond reminiscences, from 60 years ago, from people who lovingly recount their special trips to eat Mother's ice cream. It only cost 5 cents a scoop! Mother also put all of the flavors in one pint containers at 30 cents each, or 4 for a dollar.

Holly Hill Dairy

Holly Hill Dairy

The processing room was only 20 feet away from where the cows were being milked. Everything was under one roof. This new arrangement required more diligence than before. Daddy had bought a new electric bottle washer. Three bottles at a time went in as three bottles came out the other end. One day, as Bobby and Emul, a Polish immigrant who helped out for a time, were loading and unloading the bottle washer Bobby got two of the fingers on his right hand caught between the bottle and the metal bar on the machine. Emul quickly reached for a wrench, breaking the bottle to release Bobby's hand. Thank the Lord, Bobby was spared serious injury.

As soon as we were able, we all worked on the dairy farm. Billy and Bobby worked outside and in the barn, helping with the milking and other farm essentials. Kay and Radford worked in the processing area, pasteurizing and homogenizing the milk, washing bottles, and selling milk and ice cream to the customers. We ran a small, family dairy and we had 20 flavors. Like everything else in our lives, making the ice cream was a routine, a rigid process that never changed. Kay can tell it best, but we always made the vanilla first. Then we'd move on to the fruitier flavors, like strawberry, raspberry and even coffee and Tuti-Fruti. Chocolate was always last. It had to be. If we made the chocolate too early, the other flavors would all have hints of cocoa in it. Working a dairy is a true team effort. It certainly was for us.

Dairy life is a demanding life, the type of existence that

Flomich house

most people simply cannot handle. Daddy was always on-the-go, always full throttle. Harrell Bishop was truly a "man's man," a driven worker who gave his all every day, fueled by an intense desire to take care of his family and his faith in God. Kay knows about Daddy's daily routine. She was the one who had to wake him up at 2 P.M. for the afternoon milking. Rest was almost unheard of, certainly hard to come by. It was hard on all of us, but there was never any doubt that it was Daddy's show and we were just the supporting cast.

It's all a delicate balancing act, especially for dairies which processed their own milk, as we did. It all synchs up: the amount of bottles you need to have thoroughly washed clean daily, the volume of milk to be bottled, the number of butter molds, the cows that needed to be bred, the cows that needed to rest after giving birth, the rotation of the cows into their grazing field, into the milking area, and into their waiting area in the afternoons, the time to butcher cows when they're past their milk years, the minute by minute accounting of labor. It's all a part of it. Everything is constantly in motion. Theoretically, it's a stable, normalized motion which runs on predictability, but life doesn't always work that way. Unpredictable things happen. Life happens. Here's a good example. One time, 500 gallons of thick, syrupy molasses spilled all over the dairy. The cows loved it…Daddy not so much. It was like a Biblical Plague. That stuff went everywhere and it was impossible to clean up. We tried to bury it. We tried to heap sand on it. We tried to sop it up with the world's largest biscuit (not true). That's an extreme example, but it proves the point. A strict regiment is the plan. It works most of the time.

Our daily dairy life was neatly divided into two parts: morning and afternoon. Unlike suburban drive-time 6:30 A.M. morning, when we say the word "morning" on the farm, we mean it. Morning means well before the sun comes up. They were then fed in the afternoons. They spent every evening in the sand lot. They were moved every morning at 2 A.M.

Growing up "dairying" was a recurring lesson in thrift. Everything has its use on a dairy farm or a cattle enterprise, sometimes multiple uses. You plant the grass. You graze the cows on the grass. They eat the grass. That leads to their producing milk. You even save the leftovers, and cows' leftovers come in manure form.

We were able to attend college because of cow manure. It may sound a little disgusting to modern ears, but it was the final part of the process. We spent a lot of time gathering cow patties. They were used as a highly-effective fertilizer then, necessary in the sandy Florida soil, so we Bishops, with our waste-not-want-not family ethos, collected the patties. Bagging the manure was Billy and Bobby's job. They would collect the patties, bag them and then set the bags next to our old palm tree, where buyers would collect them and pay us 50 cents a bag, decent money considering that it's animal poop. Billy and Bobby even got into a memorable manure fight one day when some cousins from Georgia were visiting. The cousins, unfamiliar with farm life, sat on the fence and watched Billy and Bobby tossing cow patties at each other with pitchforks and boyish glee. We made sure that they had some good stories to tell when they returned home.

It's not only dairymen's lives that follow the pattern. Cows' lives are just as regimented, probably more so since cows rarely take vacations and have such bad table manners that they never get invited to eat at restaurants. We had one hundred cows and each one birthed one calf a year. Cow production is based on a nine-month gestation process, with a little rest time between pregnancies. Bulls would be brought in to stud, or breed, with the cows, when it was the proper time to do so. Billy got to be an expert at breeding cattle. Sometimes the bull doesn't "finish," and Billy got to be so good at recognizing the signs that he could tell if the act took place from just looking at the way the cow stands afterward. He can still perform that little bit of farm magic to this day.

The Bishop Dairy's milking system allowed for 12 cows on each side of the barn, divided by the feed trough, a state-of-the-art practice at the time. At the Holly Hill Dairy we had a new milking machine with a half-door entrance. Three cows would be herded into their proper places, one behind the other, in a row. This technology has progressed quite a bit over the years, from its beginnings as a man tying one cow to a post and hand-milking into a bucket to organized agri-business with thousands of cows and massive machinery to milk them. At Holly Hill we had a three-cow-in-a-tandem-row system. It worked like clockwork. We herded the cows into their positions and fixed them in place. Then we hooked their udders into the milking machine, one by one. By the time the third cow had her udders in the machine the first cow had finished its milking. It was three minutes per cow, three cows at a time, making for a continuous motion of 3-3-3. From each milking machine the milk was moved, via a pipe, to the cooler tank.

Dairies produce milk and butter. We made more than just that, but those are the basics for any dairy operation. There are some more detailed dairy facts in the appendix of this book, but here's a highly abridged summary: you feed and take care of the cows, you milk them, and you process the milk so that you end up with milk and butter.

Butter comes from separating the butter fat from the pasteurized milk. Before the idea that all butter should come in a rectangular stick got firmly lodged in the minds of American consumers, butter often came in different shapes. We used to put our butter into one-pound molds that resembled upside-down cakes.

Besides the standard milk and butter, we innovated and delighted tourists and Daytona children with ice cream. Did they all scream for ice cream?

Yes, a few of them did, in fact, scream for ice cream. Kay was in charge of the ice cream. She often wound up screaming AT the ice cream. The ice cream production process sounds so simple when you type it out, but in reality it was anything but simple. It was difficult, regimented, labor-intensive, and it wound up destroying the simple childhood joy of ice cream for Kay. I'm sure Willy Wonka eventually wound up feeling the same way about chocolate.

Since we were not only next to the bustle of Daytona, but also in the middle of Florida farm country, farmers would bring us fresh fruit and eggs, to name just a few. We, being a dairy family with a waste-not/want-not attitude, incorporated their foods into what we sold to the public. Unlike a large dairy conglomerate, or a chain like Baskin Robbins, we made it all fresh. That's what people wanted and expected in those days. It's sad that

America has all but lost its taste for fresh food, but we're proud to have been a part of it.

It was the same routine every week. We'd start with vanilla on Monday. It's the baseline for ice cream. It's the simplest to make. We could make a lot of vanilla ice cream and then gradually add to it over the course of the week, until, as always, we ended the week with chocolate. The schedule was set by how often we had to wash out the flavor from the vat. All the fruity flavors would be made on the same day each week. All of the nutty flavors would be created on a different day. The always-interesting, rarely exactly the same, "tuti-fruti" fruit blend would be the end result of the various fruit flavors we'd created on fruit day. We even made eggnog occasionally, adding the eggnog blend into our ready-made ice cream.

There are so many strange and memorable aspects of our fresh ice cream production process that we likely don't remember them all. For example, we had to use overripe bananas for the banana flavor. It's strange how individually they don't taste right until they've ripened, but they're perfect for ice cream. We had a local rabbi come to the dairy to bless the milk so that we were able to serve kosher milk, so we may, at some point, have actually made kosher ice cream. We even bridged American religious divides with our ice cream.

The ice cream screamers came in waves. In the morning there was usually a wave. Around 9 or 10 AM it slowed down. The early afternoons gave us the biggest waves of screamers. It was ice cream, so, naturally, we served a lot of children, but a surprising number of adults loved it, too. We'd advertise the flavors of the day on our wooden menu board outside alongside the other dairy offerings, so that customers could decide if they wanted some ice cream along with their milk order.

According to Kay, "The worst part of waiting on customers was that so many people didn't clean their bottles. I hated to see those people who brought their bottles back, with their mold, their chocolate residue. We had a lot of regulars, so after a while you knew who was dirty and who wasn't. I'd see the dirty ones walking up and I wanted to…" One of the more disgusting aspects of running a dairy was washing the old glass bottles. We were better environmentalists back then, despite what the history books say and what the younger generation thinks. It may have been better for the planet, but it was labor-intensive.

If there were an Eleventh Dairy Commandment, it would be this: Thou shalt not waste a drop of milk. To a dairyman, pouring even a droplet of milk down the drain is an unpardonable sin. Nothing is wasted. The only time a dairyman pours milk down a drain or empties a bucket of milk into a field is when the milk is spoiled, and that's not something that you can afford to let happen on a dairy.

When we did wind up with an excess of milk, we traded it to another Port Orange dairy. They did the same with us. We'd load ten-gallon metal cans on the back of the pick-up truck with a dolly, cover them with a tarp, and haul them to another dairy.

Yes, technically the other dairies were our competition, but as cattlemen we were also all in the same boat, so to speak. There's a brotherhood.

We all recall the time that Bobby, as a teenager, thought he was stronger and smarter than Daddy's system. He thought that he was as strong as Daddy, at least powerful enough to wheel a drum on its round bottom ridges over to the pick-up and therefore not have to use the dolly. But Bobby's grand plans for innovation came to a screeching halt when he found out how heavy those drums are. His crashed, and ten-gallons of precious milk spilled onto the floor. Bobby had violated the Dairyman's Eleventh Commandment. It's the kind of hubris-fueled, youthful mistake that you only make once on a dairy.

We sold half-gallon glass bottles of milk. This was a time before the big producers started putting milk in cartons. Nowadays, since the country has developed a sense of environmentalism (something that farmers and dairymen have always known), milk is beginning to move back toward bottle-standard. Our prices were reasonable and stable. It would cost you 45 cents for a bottle of pasteurized milk. It was 47 cents for homogenized milk. Ice cream was a bargain at 5 cents a scoop, and most customers chose the double scoop for ten cents. We were right off of Highway US-1, near the, then-under-construction I-95, so we had an ideal location for people just to drop by and get some ice cream for their children. The truck route passed right by us for three years while the interstate was being built.

While Daddy ran the dairy, Momma ran the retail and the ice cream production. She helped out with the indoor part of the production process, too, but she also had a home to manage. She had help, but it was her department. She bought the few groceries we couldn't grow or make. We had a vegetable garden. We sold bread at the store, along with eggs and a few other non-dairy items, too.

We didn't, however, own a washing machine or a dryer. Momma took weekly trips to the washateria, now commonly called the Laundromat, before hanging all of our wet clothes out "on the line" to dry. She was also in charge of cleaning. Above and beyond normal cleaning, working dairies need to be sparklingly clean. Bacteria are always waiting for their chance to invade, and so you have to be vigilant. When Momma felt that Tide brand detergent had gotten too expensive, she switched to BK Powder, a terrible, horrific, cheap, scouring, cleaning powder which was strong enough to clean elephant outhouses, but too strong for children's clothes. One day in school, right after Momma had switched to BK Powder, Billy's rear end started itching so badly that he was sure that he'd caught some life-threatening butt disease. It was just the detergent, but it's still funny.

The Bishop family work ethic has kept us all going, through lean times and good times. Our parents always wanted to give us the opportunity to have choices in life. We three agree that they did a good job. We learned the value of work early on. Besides working at the dairy, we did plenty of other jobs to earn a buck. We learned quickly in junior high school that we could earn good money finding lost golf balls and gathering up the brightly-colored range balls at the Riviera Golf Course north of our place. Heck, we made $50-$60 a week at the golf course. We only earned a $5/week allowance at the dairy. That was a large allowance for children in those days, but trust us when we say that we earned every penny.

Yes, we worked a lot as adolescents, but it wasn't all toil and back ache. We were still kids, and around Daytona Beach was a pretty great place to grow up. Even on the dairy, we were never really all that far from the beach, even when it seemed like a whole different world. Billy and Bobby played on Little League baseball teams every year. (Baseball is more popular in Florida than it is in the rest of the South. The weather is perfect for baseball. Also, Florida had and has a larger immigrant population from baseball-loving areas, and baseball is a popular pastime on the Caribbean islands and in South America, all of which are closer to Florida in latitude and temperament than to, say, Arkansas.)

Our neighbor, Mrs. Waters, an ardent gardener with a pristine yard, was not too fond of Billy and Bobby as boys. She took a lot of pride in keeping her yard looking perfect. It would've been perfect, too, if it weren't for Billy, Bobby and baseball season. They hit baseballs into her yard so often that it might as well have been a batting cage. She should have charged us for ball rental. The boys knew that hitting a ball into Mrs. Waters' yard had the same result as hitting one into the ocean. She never gave those balls back. We're sure that she's since passed a warehouse of old baseballs down to her children and grandchildren, Billy and Bobby hit so many of them her way.

There was a group of seven or eight boys in our Holly Hill neighborhood when we were little. They'd come and work for Daddy some, but Billy and Bobby remember play more than work. The boys would play marbles. They'd fish. They'd play baseball or football. Boys will be boys no matter where they live.

The worst whoopin' Billy ever got had to have been what made his sense of cattle-breeding so keenly-honed. It was football season and Billy wanted to get off work and play ball with the neighborhood boys, but first he was supposed to breed one of the many cows to one of the few bulls. Daddy knew that Billy was a fast breeder, but even the best ones don't bat a thousand. Daddy yelled for Billy to breed #31 to A-91 (We don't actually recall the exact numbers—it has been a few decades.). Billy grabbed a cow near #31 and bred her to the bull. But Billy had grabbed #33, who wasn't ready to mate. It was too early for #33. When Daddy discovered what had happened, he took off his old, leather belt and chased Billy around in a circle, finally catching him and giving him the worst whipping Billy ever got. Like we said, Daddy wasn't cruel, but he was practical. He wanted to teach us responsibility. Breeding a cow too early can kill her. It can ruin her milk production for life. It's a sin right below dumping good milk onto the ground.

Sargeant's Store was the downfall of many a Holly Hill boy. The little general store was right behind our barn. We could sneak out the back of the feed barn and go to the store without being seen. In retrospect, Daddy should have put up a brick wall, or had us low-jacked. We snuck over to the store every chance we got, especially after they put in a pinball machine. These were the days before people had video game systems in their homes, well before people had games available on their own phones. Pinball was a big deal. It was one of those pinball machines which let you win free games if you scored enough points. We got so good that one of us should've considered a career as a professional pinball wizard. When we heard Daddy's rubber boots scrape across the floor of Sargeant's Store, we knew that we were busted.

Then there was the time that Bobby had had enough of his dairy chores. Billy was probably the man behind this plan, in some aggravating way. That day, at 12 years old, Bobby marched right up to Daddy while he was washing down the milking parlor one Saturday afternoon, and announced, in an assertive tone of voice, "I quit." Daddy didn't say a thing. He didn't yell at Bobby. He just calmly reached for the rubber hose that was used in the milking machine vacuum line and quickly repurposed the hose, applying it to Bobby's rear end repeatedly. After a round and round routine very familiar to both Billy and Bobby, Bobby rapidly made his exit, back to the manure job he had so abruptly left, never again to raise the issue of quitting.

One steadying influence in our childhoods was our religion, or rather, our faith in God, as learned and practiced through our Baptist upbringing.

Faith in God has always been one of the cornerstones of our lives. Our foundation is firm, fixed upon Jesus Christ, the Son of God. As kids, we were members of the First Baptist Church in Daytona Beach. Due to the necessities of morning work on a dairy farm, Daddy could never attend Sunday morning services. He went to some of the night services, though. Momma, on the other hand, used to lead our "Coming Together Classes" and was Superintendent of the Jr. Children's Department. She always played "Jesus, Lover of my Soul," the only hymn she could play, on the piano. Teaching the children the books of the Bible, their order, their lessons and their importance, was one of her teaching goals. She succeeded, as we did, finally, absorb those many lessons and are all now committed Christians ourselves.

Church is a little different in a tourist town. In the 20th century, families often attended church services even when they were on vacation…and, when they did, First Baptist was usually where they ended up. This was normal for Daytona Baptists. Our pastor would ask the congregation if there was anyone there today from Ohio, and a group of red-faced, sun-baked Ohioans would stand up. Then he'd ask if there was anyone from Indiana, and so on. We were able to meet people from all kinds of different places every single Sunday. It's important to learn how to talk to new people in this life, and we learned that lesson from a very young age.

When we moved to Oconee County one of the biggest decisions we had to make was where to attend church. In Georgia there were many Baptist churches from which to choose. Even though we were accustomed to a large city church, Daddy felt that we should go to church in the community where we lived. Released from the rigors of dairy life, Daddy was now free to attend Sunday morning services with the rest of us. He even became a deacon.

Our spiritual and religious roots are firmly grounded in the Southern Baptist tradition. Traveling missionaries, Christians who had spread the Good Word to all corners of the globe, came to our churches, including many Lottie Moon missionaries, named after the noted Southern Baptist missionary who spent forty years in China.

Our faith grounded us as kids. No matter where we were traveling in our teenage fantasy lives, the church always brought us back to reality. We tithed ten percent of our allowances to the church weekly, as our parents taught us. Much as the money helped to make us feel like we were a part of the process of the dairy, our tithing and going to church made us feel like we were a part of the much-grander process of the human race. We stayed in the church as adults. Kay was heavily involved with the BSU

Daddy in Haiti 1980's

(Baptist Student Union) in college.

What it means to be a Southern Baptist hasn't changed much since the mid-nineteenth century. The same can't be said of other denominations. That means that, as it was then, so it is now. Sundays are still sacred Sabbath days. The Shamorck pool that we built in connection with the recreation center doesn't open on Sunday until after standard church hours. We had to debate whether or not it would be considered sacrilegious to play baseball on Sunday afternoons. Kay says, "Even today I still feel guilty about certain things on Sundays." Even going out to eat on The Lord's Day is a tough decision, since it might deprive waiters and cooks from getting to go to their own churches.

Being a dedicated Baptist means that we have traveled to places we never would have otherwise, and helped make them just a little better. Volunteering for mission trips is something we've always done. Mama felt strongly that heeding the call to be a missionary was our Christian duty. Though we've been to Jamaica, Romania, Guatemala and many other countries around the world, the place which left the strongest impression on our hearts has to be Haiti. You haven't seen poverty until you've seen Haitian poverty. The sense of complete desperation visible on the faces of the people will haunt you until your dying day. We went to Haiti to work with orphans and generally minister however we were able. We built buildings. We fed hungry children. We played games with them. There were just so many orphaned children that it made your heart ache. One day in Haiti we were tasked with digging a hole for a septic tank. The mission organizers dropped us off in the woods with the plan and some tools. We were going to just dig the hole ourselves. We're a cattle family. We're used to physical labor. But, within an hour of being dropped off we found ourselves surrounded by 30 skinny Haitians begging us to let them work. Deciding on the most Christian manner of solving this dilemma, we cut a deal with them, giving each of them $20/day to dig the perfect hole. The Catholic authorities down there didn't like us to pay the Haitians, but those guys worked for it. They deserved their pay. "We just don't know how fortunate we are." It's something we all say and know deep-down as truth after seeing what life is like in Haiti.

Our Christian faith is important to us. It's a legacy we desire to pass on to the next generation. Being steeped in the "Old Time Religion" ourselves, our faith has permeated our lives and given us purpose. Our generation has simply picked up the torch passed to us by our ancestors. Mama's grandfather was a circuit preacher. Our grandmother Eva used to sing at his services. Along with the dairy, Christianity has been a constant and reassuring presence, every day of the week, not merely on the seventh. This trajectory has meant inviting the preacher over to your house for Sunday dinner when it is your turn in the rotation, joining in on the outreach efforts, and living the faith in our daily lives.

The Baby Boomer era (post WWII-1960) changed our family fortune drastically. In 1945 there were 25 or 26 dairies in Volusia County, Florida, our county. By 1960, just fifteen years later, there were only three. The larger dairies had bought up the smaller ones or had run them out of business. Also, the new "convenience" stores, like 7-11 had begun to move into the area and undercut the locals by selling milk, eggs, bread and ice cream cheaper than we ever could. It's called it "lost leader" pricing. The national chains could afford to temporarily lose a little money on some products, in order to make more in the long run. Daddy was faced with the prospect of retooling the entire production process, moving from glass bottles to the popular, new wax milk containers. Nobody reused the wax containers, and so we would've lost a vital link in the chain of production. (We used to pay 15 cents for each milk bottle returned to us.) Instead of going through the expensive headache of switching to plastic, we decided instead to close up shop and move the family north instead of facing the unstoppable juggernaut of change that was threatening us in Daytona Beach.

Daddy had always in his plans to retire early. He wanted to return to his boyhood home area in northeast Georgia. When two farms became available to buy in Watkinsville our parents knew this was where they wanted to retire, and so they did. They used the land to start a beef cattle farm.

The mid-20th century changed America from a largely-agrarian nation with independent cities and townships into an industrialized powerhouse with interconnected states. Interstates linked the country. Air travel became cheaper and more accessible to more people. Businesses consolidated. Big fish gobbled up the little fish. The days of the rural ice cream stand were coming to an end. We had survived a lot of changes, but realists follow the advice of the great Kenny Rogers, and "Know when to hold 'em/Know when to fold 'em." We folded in the 60's, but we were still a family of dairymen. We didn't quit. It wasn't in our nature to quit. We just moved to Georgia.

The Georgia Farm

CHAPTER FOUR

THE SOUTHERN PIEDMONT

written by our very own family geographical professional, William "Billy" Bishop

Our farm lies in the Southern Piedmont geographical province of the United States...more specifically, the midland slope of the Washington Plateau of the Southern Piedmont of the United States. This 150-miles band that runs between the Coastal Plain and the Northern Piedmont is one of the best places on Earth to live.

The most distinctive feature of the Southern Piedmont is the gently rolling terrain with its hundreds of streams, creeks and rivers. This gives "the land" that three-dimensional visual perception so exemplified by our farm. It is somewhat magnified by the original cotton cropland terraces that still remain today.

The Southern Piedmont, or S.P., is also known for its four distinct seasons. Winters are mild. Spring and fall are beautifully-colored. The Appalachian Mountains (of which range we are at the southernmost base) and the Gulf Stream also contribute to the relatively mild winters, at least compared to the harshness of winters further north. There is never any doubt as to what time of the year it is on our farm.

The geographic location of the Southern Piedmont gives it a distinct advantage as an area for raising cattle. Warm weather grasses (such as Bermuda grass or Bahia) will not thrive, nor even grow, further north. The opposite is true of winter grasses (like Fescue, Orchard, or Rye), which will neither grow nor thrive south of the Southern Piedmont. And, what do cattle love? Grass. They love grass, and the Southern Piedmont is highly adaptable, with land easily able to a switch to nearly any type of grass, no matter how rare. On our farm Fescue and Bermuda grass pastures allow grazing all year long.

The Southern Piedmont is the "birthplace" for the headwaters for numerous watersheds that flow through to the Coastal Plain. Thus, all of the S.P. is bisected by numerous waterways, which give the region an abundance of flowing water.

On our farm (414 acres) there are two branches (the Back Branch and the Bishop Branch), and Calls Creek (the southern boundary), as well as two spring-fed ponds. This allows for plenty of running water to serve as a drinking source for the cattle.

To compliment this is the prevalence of high-quality sub-surface ground water (the well). On the farm we have six wells (four of them are active), all of which produce high volumes of water, serving the pools (Shamrock), a subdivision (KW), and all of the farm's dwellings and facilities.

Location, location, location. The Southern Piedmont has it all. The farm is surrounded by the best and biggest lakes in Georgia: Hartwell, Lanier, Sinclair, Clark Hill and Russell. They're all located in the S.P. and are all only an hour's drive from the farm. Not much farther away (2 and ½ hours) is the Atlantic Coast and all of the amenities it provides.

Further enhancing all this abundance is the University of Georgia, only six miles away. Athens provides a great atmosphere for a major college town. Athletic events, cultural events, and all of the other activities that UGA offers make being so close to the campus highly desirable.

Agriculture in the Southern Piedmont is so significant that the U. S. Department of Agriculture established a research farm in Oconee County in 1937. Located adjacent to our farm, the benefits of this have been numerous. Included among these are: the availability of new farming techniques, high quality hay, and breeding seed stock. It's all literally right across the street.

In summary, the Southern Piedmont is a great place to live, especially in Oconee County. We have it all: a beautiful land-scape, wonderful climate, an abundance of water for agricultural pursuits and well as recreation, a great location in relation to the mountains, the coast, Atlanta, and the University of Georgia.

Indeed, Oconee County of the Southern Piedmont has been recognized by many as being one of the best places to live, and raise cattle, in all of America.

Mother and Daddy's Georgia Home 1960

CHAPTER FIVE

THE BLACK CONNECTION

also written by Billy

Daddy and Mama had made the big decision to sell the dairy and move to Georgia and start a cattle farm. The next important decision they were faced with was what beef cattle breed to use.

Other important decisions had already been made: the location of the farm, picking a new house plan, what church to attend. However, selecting a breed was essential and was a process they made over several years.

Being a dairy farmer, Daddy had been devoted to the Guernsey breed and totally understood the characteristics of genetics.

The annual Volusia County Fair was held in Deland, Florida, not too far from the dairy. It afforded us an excellent opportunity to compare and analyze the different breeds of livestock being shown in competition, side by side. On at least three occasions Daddy and I attended the competition, which was usually held on Friday afternoon and often lasted into the night. Daddy would spend this time talking with competitors (the men, not the cows) about their particular breeds. Although there were many breeds to choose from (Hereford, Shorthorn, Charolais, Santa Gertrudis, Angus), Daddy eventually whittled it down to either Charolais or Angus.

Charolais white cattle were becoming very popular and were considered to be a warm-climate breed. (Charolais is a breed of beef cattle from the Charolais region surrounding Charolles, in Burgundy, in eastern France.) Angus, on the other hand, was thought to be a Northern breed, a cattle persuasion which had not infiltrated the South, as had the Charolais. (Black Angus originally came from the counties of Aberdeenshire and Angus in Scotland.) At the time, it was generally believed that black cattle, like Angus, would not do well in hot climates. This, of course, turned out not to be the case at all, as our family and history have proven.

After several years of study and observation, Daddy had finally decided to go with the Black Angus. He purchased two Angus bulls and in 1958 or 1959 we began crossbreeding the dairy cows with the Angus bulls, thus creating the herd which would later stock the farm in Georgia.

White face Hereford cattle were far and away the dominant breed in the South, especially in Oconee County. Other than ours, there were virtually no black cattle in the county, although the USDA experiment station in Watkinsville was beginning to introduce and research Angus in the late 1950's.

In choosing the Angus breed, Daddy was not only going against the conventional wisdom, but also against what cattlemen in Oconee County were doing every day. He saw the future once again. As he had so many times before, Daddy was taking the road less traveled…and that has made all the difference.

What a decision it was! Our calves always brought top prices and the black cattle thrived in the Southern Piedmont. Even more important was that, over time, the Angus breed produced the best premium beef and now all high-quality restaurants proudly advertise in their menus that they serve "Certified Angus Beef." The tenderness, flavor and unique marbling of Angus cattle fed on Bermuda grass is universally recognized as superior beef, when compared to other breeds or to unnatural grain-fed factory cattle. Once again, Daddy had proven himself to be a pioneer and an innovator.

Today, in Georgia and elsewhere, Black Angus cattle are not only prominent, but they are by far the dominant breed in the U.S.A. For over 50 years we have raised Black Angus cattle. Hopefully, we can continue the "Black Connection" for another 50 years!

CHAPTER SIX

THE UNIVERSITY OF GEORGIA:
GO DAWGS!

The University of Georgia has played a large role in all of our lives. We've learned our future crafts there. We've watched as the University of Georgia expanded its reach into our once-placid agricultural county. We've rooted for the Bulldogs. Our parents' premonition about the happiness that this area could bestow upon our family, an idea they silently conceived almost a full century ago, has come true in many ways, some expected, some utterly surprising. We Bishops are a Bulldog family. Like the routine rigors of dairy work, the steadfast teachings of the Southern Baptist Church, and our ancestors' traditional American work ethic, our interactions with the University of Georgia has shaped us all.

We've already written about the different effects on our lives of living in a tourist town versus a more rural, farm community. We've mentioned how important our father believed that education was for his children. We've touched on the fact that Oconee County is a sort of hybrid suburban college town, with elements of a traditional agricultural community blended with the amenities that UGA and Athens as a whole affords its residents. Now we'd like to spell out exactly what UGA has meant to us.

Education was important to our parents. It's important to us. And, therefore, it will continue to be important to future generations of Bishop (and Shepard) children. Our parents were not able to graduate from college. They were certainly intelligent enough, but harsh circumstances prevented them from doing so. They made sure that trend ended with their generation. Mama and Daddy championed the value of knowledge. Daddy noticed that his classmates who had college degrees were given more opportunities in life than those without them. He always maintained that, "Once you get a college education you can never have it taken away from you." You can lose money. You can lose land. You can lose hope, and love, and dreams. But if you're educated, you're educated for life. All of their children and grandchildren have earned 4-year and advanced degrees.

Education's benefits are many and varied: from being able to properly fill out a crossword puzzle to higher wages. Generally speaking, the more degrees one has the more money one will make in his or her profession. You can see this principle at work in the corporate world, the agricultural world, even the military. The difference between NCOs (Non-Commissioned Officers) and military officers is simple---the officers graduated from college. That's it. Without a degree a soldier can only be promoted so far. Without a degree there's a ceiling. Like many aspects of life, it's easier to see in the military, but it's true everywhere. Billy and Bobby both went through ROTC. Bobby stayed in the military for two years afterward. Military life taught them discipline and life skills, but also helped the family pay for college. Billy's geographical knowledge gave him a leg up in ROTC. Most of his classmates couldn't even read a map. Bobby studied engineering both in the military and in college. Education has helped us in ways we couldn't have predicted with a crystal ball, in ways our ancestors couldn't have even fathomed.

We even sold a portion of our Oconee farm to a college

which is presently known as The University of North Georgia (a combination of what was formerly Truett-McConnell and Gainesville College). One of our neighbors is a college. We rarely ask them to borrow sugar, but they're good neighbors to have, and the college's presence makes us all feel as if we're fulfilling our parents' dream every time we look over and see bright-eyed young people coming over to our land to learn skills which will help our state grow and prosper. Many of Truett's students were adults who took classes at night while working during the day. They've seen what American life is like without a college degree and took bold steps to better themselves.

We've watched this little school grow and expand from a store front in the Bell's shopping center to a group of spill-over trailers, to the proper campus they occupy. In 1982, the local

Truett-McConnell satellite "campus" was operating out of the old local high school. It was a tiny operation then, with a first class of just six students. Once the Bell's Shopping Center was built, the classes moved down the street and into some of the adjoining store-fronts, with the student body steadily growing to the point that the school was soon spilling out into the trailers behind the Bell's grocery store anchor building, essentially forming a mobile classroom. It was an area to learn, but not a very good one. Something had to be done. We, being right down the road and being concerned citizens of the county, eager to see the area thrive, watched the development of Truett-McConnell with interest.

With the school's rapid expansion, we came up with the idea of offering land to the school, agreeing to slice off a decent-sized chunk, a 14-acre tract, of the farm to build a real campus for this scrappy little college. Kay led the way. As an educational insider, she was the family's link to the wants and needs of the school. We offered Truett-McConnell a sweetheart deal, a business decision that would pay off for everyone involved. We even built the first building ourselves. Later, Gainesville Junior College bought and took over the campus, but it remained essen-

Groundbreaking Truett-McConnell College 11/7/1993

tially the same school with the same mission, on the same tract of our land.

Helping local people enhance their lives, moving up a rung or two on society's ladder by furthering their education at night, while still being able to work and take care of their families during the day was just one way that we've managed to continue to act as stewards of the land, even in this, the Digital Age. The school catered mainly to what they classify as "non-traditional students," adults who, for one reason or another, are going back to school later in life. It's a motel campus, focusing on education rather than campus life, but, with our help, it's gotten progressively more traditionally college-like, adding facilities when it's been financially able to do so, often with our aid and direction. During the early growth years many family members contributed to the success of the college by teaching, advising, cleaning and managing the campus bookstore. Many students use the college as "back-door" entrance to the University of Georgia. As we write this (in January of 2016), the college has been incorporated into the University of North Georgia and has a student body of 2500, plus over 100 faculty members. Its teacher/student ratio is enviable, keeping class sizes small and manageable, ensuring that its students get the individual attention they need to learn a new trade.

As a career educator and academic advisor, Kay has helped shepherd (no name pun intended) many students into the college, through it, and then transfer to another school or out into the world. It's been a ministry as much as a center of higher learning. According to Kay, "I've never had a student finish here who didn't get into Georgia." With UGA's ever-increasing entrance standards, that's saying something. We're all proud of what we've accomplished with this school, none of us more so than Kay.

There are now around 2200 UNG students and over 10,000 applicants each year. As you can tell, it's a big source of pride for us.

We all value knowledge, but, if we're being honest, Kay's love of education probably wins out in this, our generation of Bishops. Education has been Kay's calling, her profession. She's taught half of Oconee County. She's counseled the area's teenagers and thrown them a loving rope to help guide them through the choppy waters of adolescence.

CHAPTER SEVEN

GROWTH YEARS

Lived on and around it…

Cultivated it…

Pruned it…

Live off of it…

Improved it…

Harvested (developed) it…

Maintained it…

Preserved it…

Shared it…LAND!

Being faithful stewards of the land has become something of a Bishop family creed, a living oath, not simply some pabulum that we repeat, but something we've lived, something we learned, and something we intend to pass on.

It's all true. Our parents and we have lived on and around

the land, building homes and farms. We've cultivated the pastures. We've pruned a lot of it, cutting timber, constructing and using hay barns, among other activities. We've lived off of the land, eating the cattle as well as selling them. We've harvested/developed it, allowing worthwhile local endeavors, like the bank, AT&T, the Department of Transportation (DOT) and Truett-Mc-Connell College to use parts of the land to set up shop, while insuring that they keep the basic feel of, the structure of, the land before it was developed. We've maintained it with constant perseverance. We've preserved it, with the bulk of it being used for cattle and the farm still present. And we've shared it, allowing it to be used for family gatherings, weddings and events.

As Billy says about the land, "It's like somebody has put you in charge of something. You just try to preserve and maintain it. It's your charge." It has been our charge. We've heeded the call. Since then we've discovered alternative uses for the farm land, while still holding onto the spirit of the land instilled in us by our parents. Or, to put it another way, "We started eating this hog one leg at a time. Since the 70's, he's down to just two legs, but he's still hanging in there."

Along with the subdivision and the recreation center/pool, we've engaged ourselves in a number of other side projects. They're literally side projects, coming as they have on the sides of our land.

The first leg of the proverbial hog we sliced off to roast was

Shamrock Recreation Club

the Killarney West subdivision we built in the 1970's on the western side of our farm. Later, in 1991-92, we offered Truett-McConnell Junior College 14 acres on the eastern side of the farm. A
few years later we struck a deal with AT&T (the phone company)
and the federal D.O.T. (Department of Transportation) built the
U.S. Highway 441 by-pass road through the eastern side of the
farm. In 1999, we offered a piece of land to the First American
bank (provided they didn't cut down the beautiful and beloved,
century-old Magnolia Tree). Our struggles with the D.O.T. are
representative of this new phase of farm usage we'd entered into.
Being a federal government department, the Transportation hon-
chos used their, rather authoritarian, power of Eminent Domain
to essentially rob us of our property rights, but that didn't mean
that we were just going to let them roll over us. Still fighting for

stewardship of the farm, we wrangled with them, just like we wrangled with AT&T (when that powerful company thought they could simply dictate terms to we simple farm folk, incorrectly guessing that, with all of their money, power, and political influence, we wouldn't fight them) until all parties came to an equitable arrangement.   That's the basic timeline, the bare-bones series of events, but that's not the end of the story.

All of these developments were evidence that a wise and an economically-advantageous investment in land, over a 50-year cycle, can produce in real dollars-and-cents, a lesson we learned from our parents.

As we've said, in 1972 we helped to develop a subdivision on the western edge of the land, and named it Killarney West.

Gene and Billy 441 Bypass through the farm

This project took a lot of work. It even took some elbow grease, and mouth grease, just to get started. Billy had to physically travel back to Florida to convince Daddy that this was a good idea. It's turned out to be a wonderful thing, but Harrell Bishop didn't immediately take to the, at the time relatively new, idea of housing subdivisions. But Billy is nothing if not persistent. He slept on Daddy's refusal for the night and awoke the next morning to more than freshly-squeezed Florida orange juice. Daddy relented once Billy floated his idea to make the subdivision a total Bishop family project, including Bobby, Kay, and Radford in the development.

Our first step in the development of Killarney West in the 1970's was to put together a few "spec" homes. Those first spec houses were delivered by large trucks and pieced together right there on the property, where they would soon take root. The 70's was a difficult time financially. Interest rates were high. Building costs were high. The period of seemingly never-ending waiting for potential buyers to sign on the dotted line was interminable, causing more than a few gray hairs on all of our heads. But God was faithful to us, His followers, and we survived the hard times and saw the light of better days.

It was a big decision. That was the first time we'd cut off any of the property. It's as self-contained as a subdivision would need to be. Water for the subdivision comes from the newly-drilled well on the land. The country view from the houses is pleasant and calming, but also convenient for local families, close to the high school, library, and shopping centers in Watkinsville.

It was a gamble, but it worked. Oconee families would thereafter have safe, affordable, and attractive roofs over their heads. Sandy and Billy and Kay and Gene even built their own houses in the subdivision in 1974. They all still live there today, just as Bobby still lives in the original 1960 home that Daddy built in Oconee. Practicing what you preach has always been a Bishop family creed.

We built a recreational facility on the land, complete with a lighted softball field for night play, a tennis court and a pool. We set the entire Shamrock Recreation Club complex up as a "members only" enterprise in order to pay for the upkeep of the recreation facility. Go Seals! Pools are not cheap to operate. They're worth it, but they're expensive. With sports in general, and specifically baseball, having played such an important role in our past, we felt obliged to do this, to give back to a community that had welcomed us many years earlier. Although costly to set-up, the Shamrock Recreation Club helped us to stay afloat, slight pun intended, in more ways than one. Not only did we see a huge payoff in the raised quality of Oconee County life, but we even reaped actual income, which helped to off-set the time between paying to build the subdivision houses and their purchase. There's a lesson here about not putting all of your eggs in one basket. There's another lesson that cannot adequately be put into words. Being able to be the founders and caretakers of an outdoor play-ground for children and adults is priceless. By sticking our necks out yet again in service to something we love, something greater than ourselves, allowed us to witness ballgames, swim meets, and Fourth of July barbecues by merely walking out our back doors.

The private pool is something we wanted to do so that Oconee families who join us as members would have a cool place to enjoy in the summers. At the time we built it there were no pools in the area, other than a few private neighborhood pools and one pool in Bogart, but that wasn't convenient for Watkinsville. By using the land in yet another way our grandparents could never have predicted, we've provided a place for Oconee children to briefly escape the intense Georgia summer heat. There's no telling how many kids learned to swim in that pool, mostly at the insistence and under the instruction of Sandy. The number is too high to count at this point.

We waged an intense war with AT&T over their potential use of our land. They thought that they could bargain in bad faith and that we were, comparably, too small to stand up to them. They didn't know our family.

AT&T wanted to lay underground cable on the property lines across our farm, to connect phone and Internet users around the area (in the dark days before wireless connectivity). We had a deal, which they tried to break. We ultimately had to take them to court in order to protect out property. The judge found in our favor, ruling that AT&T had not negotiated in good faith, and that they would have to comply with the Bishop family's terms. We had taken the biggest phone company in America to court…and won.

We all remember another land-based battle, the one we fought against the Volusia County Tax Assessor's Office. Once our parents had moved back to Florida, they kept the basics of the dairy going, in a much more limited manner. There were still cows, but the barn was rusty, some of the sheds were falling in, some of the fence posts were rigged with tape, and the ever-present coffee weed (a fast-growing Florida staple) had overgrown to the point that it was as tall as a man's head. When the Tax Assessor visited he declared that it was no longer a bona fide working farm. Daddy disagreed. Daddy disagreed with every fiber of his being. He was still a dairy man. Although his habits hadn't changed with the times, in his heart Harrell Bishop would always be a dairy man. And who was this nameless government official to say otherwise? The family had to settle this one in court.

This court battle, a battle which, in many ways, epitomized the changes going on at the time to our nation and to our family, reached from Holly Hill to Tallahassee (the state capitol). Daddy thought that there should be exceptions, that he had justifiable reasons to exempt him from their judgment. This battle raged. There were losses and appeals. There was contention and consternation. This was, on some philosophical level, a battle for the soul of our father. Some powerful people, representatives of his own government, were telling him that he was no longer the man he'd been for decades. He could no longer call himself a cattleman. Imagine how devastating that would be.

Harrell on the Florida farm

The judge even went so far as to call our father "an anachronism," a throw-back to a previous era. In truth, Harrell Bishop was, in many ways, an anachronism. Despite what the Volusia County legal system may have thought, that's a good thing. Coming out of the Great Depression, he held on to some Depression-era values. Buying new tools was a luxury. He recycled everything. Nothing was beyond usage. He wouldn't throw away bent nails. Instead, he'd hammer them back into working shape. He, and our mother to an extent, practiced what they preached, reusing aluminum foil, 2x4s, everything.

The details of the court battle are too many to spell them all out, but suffice it to say that it was lengthy, it was impactful, and it hurt our father deeply. When a judge, a member of the community so respected that we give him the power to decide our futures, tells you that the world has passed you by it's going to sting. Perhaps the world had passed him by, but he retained the positive and eternal values and beliefs of his day...and they are worth preserving for the benefit of future generations.

CHAPTER EIGHT

DRAWN BACK

In ways large and small, great and wide, minute and only noticeable to us, our parents lived the American Dream. They could have been poster children FOR the American Dream. They came from proud people, their values reflected those of the community, they were committed Christians, they worked hard, saved their money and invested wisely while they built their lasting family legacy, they worked steadfastly and enjoyed the fruits of their labor…for the sake of their family. It was always about the family.

Mother and Daddy reorganized their energy toward one another in their later years. And when they took this step, like everything else they had done in their lives, they did it right. Daddy didn't literally "lay down his tools," but he laid them down to the extent that he was able to stop working all-day, every day. Daddy was always a hard worker, and so even after he "retired" he still worked, but he was better able to enjoy the little things in life. At least in part that was because of where he and Mother moved. They were drawn back to Florida. They traveled all over the globe. They drove around the country. When Daddy went to buy a motor home, he wound up buying two.

Even after he "retired," Harrell Bishop still managed to stay on top of things in his world. He boarded horses for the city equestrian kids who had neither the room nor the facilities to keep them at their own houses. Those kids, and adults too, would come out to the dairy with smiles on their faces and log a few cherished hours in the saddle. We'd travel down to Daytona to see him and Mother and would find little yellow crayon instructions on almost everything. They were directions for what he wanted us to fix, sell or replace. "Fix this" would be scrawled onto the side of a farm implement. "Sell this" would be affixed to a piece of furniture. Daddy always managed to leave his mark. In his later years that mark was always written in yellow.

On the Florida farm

This little tale is so representative of who Harrell Bishop was that it begged us to be retold. Daddy flew to Indiana to buy a motor home. That was where they were being made, therefore that's where they would be cheapest to buy and where he could be assured of inspecting his newest purchase and being able to look the salesman in the eye and make sure the man was an honest broker. As he always did, especially for a large purchase like a motor home, Daddy had done his homework. He knew that it

was cheaper to fly to Indiana, the state where they made the motor homes, buy it and then drive it back. In the process of doing
what he always did, Daddy even managed to one-up himself. He
bought two motor homes, driving one back home himself and
getting the salesman to drive the other.

It may seem like a relatively small and unimportant incident, and it was, but it is just so representative of Harrell that
it deserves repetition. Not only did Daddy foresee the NEED to
buy two motor homes, one for him and Mother and one for the
children and grandchildren. He saw both the potential for future
family bliss and the DEAL and knew that it was too good to pass
up. Further, he was able to talk the salesman into driving three
states away and providing literal home delivery. Daddy knew how
to work capitalism to his advantage.

Although he clearly played a big role in the story of our
lives, we feel that we haven't yet accurately described our father as
a person, as a man.

Daddy never had much in the way of a personal life. He
couldn't even attend church with the rest of us, due to the con-
straints of running a working dairy. No one would ever have
accused our father of being slothful.

Our father had his harsh moments. We all got whooped
a few times growing up, mainly with Daddy's leather belt, but he
was not a cruel man. When we made mistakes as children we'd

get The Lecture. If, say, we broke something at the house, he'd tell us what we did wrong and why it was so awful, but then Daddy would always fix it. He was handy and he was always willing to lend a hand to anyone who wanted to help himself. Daddy employed a lot of otherwise unemployable workers at the dairy. Some of them rose to the occasion. More didn't. A lot of them just worked until payday and then drank their money away. But, Daddy always gave people a chance. He wasn't one to prejudge a person on a superficial snap judgment.

Harrell Bishop was a family man, always trying to incorporate the larger extended family into everything we did. Instilling in us a sense of family was one of the most important things he thought that he could teach us. And it stuck. We're even writing a book together.

Though he wasn't the person in charge of the customer service side of the operation, Daddy was always pleasant to visitors. When the sharply dressed feed salesmen would come around, Daddy would visit with them. We remember the Purina salesmen as the snappiest dressers we saw regularly on the dairy. When the city folks had finished their business and left, Daddy would often wish out loud that he'd chosen a life as an insurance salesman. It must've seemed like such an easier life to him. It probably was easier.

We don't want to give the impression that Harrell Bishop never had any fun. He'd always go to the Friday night high school football games. We had two local high schools (Seabreeze High

School for the coastal kids and Mainland High School for the inland kids), and the two schools shared a stadium, so in the fall and winter there was always a home game to attend. We were even going to attend an FSU football game against The Citadel once. That was a big deal. It was a four hour drive and we were all looking forward to it, but, of course, we had to cancel our plans to help one of the cows birth a calf. These things happen.

Daddy would also take us out to eat on Saturday nights, usually to Gardener's Seafood Restaurant, a little place his brother-in-law Russell ran. We'd get there at nine P.M., right when the stragglers from the dinner rush were all leaving to go home. Russell was a fun guy, who could "tear up" a piano, and was an avid fisherman and shrimper, which was likely why he decided to run a seafood restaurant for a living. He's the only person we know who ever fished in the flooded ditches of Willacoochee, Georgia, though we can't imagine that he actually caught anything in those rainy holes. Russell was a joker, a prankster, a funny, life-of-the-party type. One Saturday night, after he'd undoubtedly had more than a few drinks, Uncle Russell set to teasing Billy. We were eating our fresh seafood and Uncle Russell was just giving it to Billy mercilessly. Always one to respond to provocation, even as a youngster, Billy eventually reached his breaking point. Russell said one more joke and Billy got mad, grabbed a red, plastic, squeezy ketchup bottle off the table and ran around Gardener's, spraying the gooey ketchup all over the restaurant. You don't mess with Billy if you don't want to get messed with yourself.

It wasn't that Daddy wasn't a social person. At heart, he was. He just didn't have enough down time to prove it to us. In fact, we three can only recall Daddy as having one real friend in life, outside of the family, a man by the name of Eddie Gascue. Eddie's visits to the dairy were some of the only times we actually saw our father enjoy himself. Daddy and Eddie would laugh and cut up, as old friends do. Eddie Gascue was a Florida state trooper, a highway patrolman, by profession, but a baseball player at heart. He had gone to FSU, Florida State University, on a scholarship for his pitching ability. Eddie even played some Venezuelan winter league ball, before settling into his life as a policeman. Eddie's visits brought out a side of our father that we children rarely saw. Sadly, Eddie was killed by a renegade escaped fugitive while on a true old-style Florida manhunt, complete with dogs and everything, in Palmetto.

In the late 40's, Daddy bought a vacation home for Mother and himself, a 13-bedroom abandoned girls' school in the Smoky Mountains near Franklin, North Carolina, an Appalachian vacation retreat town for Florida flatlanders. Our parents fell in love with the Southern Appalachian mountains when they took their honeymoon in Tallulah Gorge in 1935. They had always nurtured that dream of retiring high up in the clouds, above the cows and their needs, above the cities and their crowds, above the farms and dairies and cars and buildings and the worry. It was a place to hold large family retreats, a place for school friends to gather, or simply a place for the nuclear family to relax and enjoy being away from the rigors of dairy life, if only for a little while. Even this restful abode came with its own challenges of upkeep and constant repair, primarily the water system. The water source was a mountain spring ½ of a mile away from the house. When

Mountain House Franklin, NC

we would arrive at our vacation home, we had to go straight to work: clearing out the winter debris at the spring house, repairing broken places in the pipes with old car tire tubes, and draining and cleaning the reservoir in the 3rd floor attic was a yearly ritual. In 1951, our former school/mountain home was host to a large, extended family retreat with Mother's family. Grandmother Summerlin and some of Mother's siblings came to the Franklin house that summer, the same year that Billy was hit by a car.

Something we could never have predicted growing up was just how much of a "character" Daddy would turn into in his later years. Before, he was almost always too busy to let his playful side out, but once he had the time, he took off his work clothes, put on his bright, solid red suit, and became something of a beloved local figure, a beloved regional character.

They also continued to spend summers in the North Carolina mountains. They wound up selling the mountain house once, but then they missed it, so they financed it, and then later sold it again. Our generation of the Bishop family has a lot of memories tied up in that house, like the summer when Daddy had dynamited too many stumps and wound up inhaling too much of the smoke (Once in Oconee, he blew up a stump using a car battery and some wires.) Another time we tried to help Daddy move an old pasteurizer vat up from Florida to the mountain house, for use as a water reservoir. We drove the 550-some miles up from Daytona to North Carolina, lugging that huge metal contraption with us. That sucker was heavy. It must have weighed at least 300 pounds, probably closer to 500 pounds, and its short legs made it even harder to maneuver. After transporting it across multiple state lines and getting it out of the truck, we then had to unload it on the tenuous and steep, 45 degree, slope of the Appalachian ridge. Even with all of us pushing and pulling, we lost and the pasteurizer won its freedom. It got away from us and started rolling down the mountain. We just watched it go on its merry way, racing downhill until it hit the ravine below. It's probably still up there somewhere, tucked away in some bushes, laughing with the other giant machines that got away about how they outsmarted their people.

The mountain folk were an interesting lot. Compared to pretty much everywhere else in the country, Appalachia has remained a fairly isolated and insulated community. In places that the never-ending wheel of American "progress" forgets, you can still find some pockets of frozen time, some rituals, behaviors, and language of an earlier era. Many of the descendents of the Scotch-Irish people who first moved into the area in the 19th century are still up there. Since it was, and still is, such an insular community, they were slow to accept new people, like us, but they quickly "took a likin'" to Daddy. He had a country background and a dairy background, and they respected that.

Mr. and Mrs. Otis Bates, the caretakers of "the big house," kept the place up for us. We enjoyed the odd ways of the native Appalachian North Carolinians, like the apologetic woman who felt bad, when we left her house, that she "Didn't have no far to give us." It took us a while to decipher that one, but eventually we figured out that she was saying the word "fire" in her heavily-accented mountain accent, and apologizing for not living up to an old custom and giving us a parting gift when we left her home. The mountain folks used to literally give their guests "fire," so that they could quickly and easily light their own fires when they reached home. That tradition carried over even past the time when "fars" were necessary. They still gave guests to their homes a little something to see them off. Mother and Daddy bought a clothes-washer for the Bates in appreciation for their "neighbor-ness." It's a beautiful gift of kindness, don't you think? Mrs. Bates was overcome with thankfulness. She had never seen an electric washer.

As we travel along the path on our respective life journeys, many of us, when we reach a certain age, a certain emotional and mental spot, feel the pull to go back to the beginning, to see where it all started. For our parents, it all started in Daytona. Their ancestors migrated to the area, and though their own migrations, with us in tow, took them to Oconee County, they couldn't shake the magnetic pull of Daytona Beach, Florida. They were drawn back in 1968.

THE PASSING OF THE TORCH

As a kid you never plan on taking over your parents' roles within the family, but it happens that way all the same. Time marches on. For us, the unspoken but vitally-important passing of the torch of Bishop family responsibility happened in the mid- to late-Sixties. This turned out to be the decade with the most life-changing events for us. This was when our larger family splintered into smaller nuclear units (we're still a very close extended family). Freed from the daily grind, our parents allowed themselves to become a couple again, enjoying a relaxed "countrypolitan" lifestyle they'd never known before. This was the time when our grandmothers both passed away. This was the time we three reluctantly turned into Georgians (well, sort of). This was the time when Daddy's business acumen took a back seat to Mama's. This was the time when our generation took over the running of the cattle farm.

America changed drastically in the 1960's, too. You couldn't be alive in that time and not see it. The president gave televised press conferences. The positive aspects of the Cold War were in full view as America raced to beat the U.S.S.R. to put a man on the moon. Many of the various parts of the country's large and expansive agriculture industries morphed into something new as well. We used to only get to eat fried chicken for Sunday dinners. It was a special meal and one that we all loved. The 60's brought us "chicken in a basket," a revolutionary new culinary concept. It sounds relatively quaint now that we've all seen it for fifty years, but the first time we Bishop kids saw crispy and juicy fried chicken cheap readily available on a Tuesday night we went crazy. The fact that we could just walk up to the counter and buy fried chicken was nothing short of miraculous. It used to take our cook, Alice, all day to fry chicken. Now we could just walk up to someone and ask for it? America's corporate progress of the 50's and 60's did radically change the running of a family dairy. The proliferation of fast-food chains and convenience stores may have spelled the end of a chapter of our lives in coastal Florida, but even we have to admit that chicken in a basket was a great invention.

Both Billy and Bobby got married in 1968. That was The Summer of Love. Looking back, apparently love was in the air for the Bishop family that year, and so were some surprises. Billy married a "double Yankee," he met while working as a camp counselor in The Poconos, the famous Pennsylvania mountains. Not only was she born and raised north of the Mason-Dixon Line, she was from New Jersey. After absorbing the shock, we all realized just how similar her upbringing had been to our own. She was from Long Branch, a beachfront community not as dissimilar from Daytona as we had first thought. The Lord works in mysterious ways. The South isn't as completely different from other areas of the country as we'd all grown up thinking.

Like we said, Oconee County never really took for Mama and Daddy. They had attempted to put down roots in Oconee, but tab A never really fit into slot B. They missed Holly Hill. They loved their Florida church. They still owned various properties in Volusia County and felt the need to be down there in order to manage and oversee their properties. Mama shined in her new role as caretaker to the Bishop family's Florida interests. They still maintained loose ties up here in north Georgia, but they also began to travel as a couple, enjoying the benefits of what they'd worked for all their lives.

Not to say that running a cattle farm is easy, but it was definitely less intense than running the dairy. We were all afforded the opportunity to travel, while still maintaining our herd and keeping our operation running smoothly. We even took a memorable family road trip out West, an iconically American type of vacation across the recently-laid asphalt interstate highways linking all corners of mainland America. Kay and Billy couldn't make that trip, but Mama, Daddy, Radford, and Bobby made it a Bishop quorum, a family trip. And, being the Bishops, we, of course, found ways to both travel on a budget AND put our ingenuity to the test. We built a box with ribs and a roof, which we then mounted on top of the green Chevy Capri station wagon, which we rode to the Rocky Mountains like our pioneering forefathers in their covered wagons. The Chevy with the box even kind of looked like a covered wagon. We drove toward the setting sun during the day, and we slept in the car and the box at night. Mama and Daddy got to sleep in the Chevy. Bobby and Radford slept in the box. Hotels are for unimaginative families.

We didn't make it all the way across the country. We did, however, make it to the Continental Divide. Considering that we had children sleeping on a roof, that's saying something.

THE SIXTIES

The decade of the 1960's has gone down in history as a time of change, an era of upheaval, ten years that forever altered the landscape of a nation. President Kennedy's youthful optimism infected all of us. We felt secure…and then came The Cuban Missile Crisis, then his assassination, then Vietnam. This decade, which had started out so hopeful, felt as if it had turned crazy practically overnight. The Bishop family went through our share of changes in that decade right along with everybody else. We sold the Holly Hill Dairy and began to settle into our new lives in Georgia. Our parents retired, slowly and gradually, and left the family business in our hands. Billy and Bobby both graduated high school, moved on to college and started families of their own. We had deaths, marriages, new friends, fresh challenges, and we all turned the page onto a new chapter of family history.

Buying two large adjacent farms and combining them into one large cattle entity made us instantly noticeable in rural Oconee County. Coming from Florida made us intriguing and the community was curious. Jumping into the scene in northeast Georgia with two feet made us a vital part of the growth of the region.

As Billy puts it, "It's one thing to move from one town to another. It's a whole other thing to move a family's life's work to another state."

There were no U-Hauls, no moving services, no help. There was just us, a 400 mile stretch of road and a few dusty pick-up trucks. Needless to say, it took us a while to move everything. We made too many trips in the first three years here to remember them all. The path of our leaving the rapid pace and ecstatic summer nights of Daytona for the greener pastures, literally, and the laid back easy-going Oconee County, took us first to Jacksonville, then from Jacksonville up GA-15 into South Georgia's cotton fields and grasslands. It was a fairly straight shot north up Georgia highway 15 in our big red truck until we reached Soperton, in central Georgia. From Soperton we continued north through Georgia's lake country, entering the Southern Piedmont region, where the land raises up and gentle hills line the horizon.

Daddy's second cousin, Ralph Green, a cotton farmer by trade, met us at the farm that first night. It was pitch black, a variety of dark we'd never known. There were no lighthouses, no boardwalk lights, no trains roaring by at all hours of the day and night. It was just dark and silent. We remember being amazed and a little scared at the lack of light and sound. The first sound we heard when we did finally arrive in Oconee County was the comforting serenade of our cattle eating our new grass. It was a good sign.

When we first moved to Oconee County, in September of 1960, there was almost nothing around us but farmland for miles in any direction. There were cotton farms and peach trees, lots of peach trees, but not much in the way of development. You knew your neighbors, which was easy since there weren't that many of them. Rayford Dawson's store was the only business we can remember being open when first the Bishops arrived in northeast Georgia. Daddy and Momma had always loved this area, having spent their honeymoon at Tallulah Gorge. Both of their sets of parents were once Georgians anyway, so when we came to Oconee County from Daytona Beach, we were really coming home.

But everything was different, including the size. The dairy had been an intense 25 acre, 100 cow operation in the middle of a town. Our new land was vast and rural. We combined what had formerly been two farms: a 195-acre farm and a 220-acre farm. To the east was the Harris farm, family cemetery and home place. To the west was the Crowley farm, which doubled as a place for the local sheriff to lay his head. We were just one mile away from US highway 441. Virtually in the center of the county, we were ½ a mile away from the new high school in one direction and ½ a mile away from the county courthouse in the other. Athens was right down the road.

You may think that we're exaggerating just how rural it was in Oconee back then. We're not. The county was home to one-tenth of its present (2016) population when we arrived. The police force consisted of a sheriff and one deputy, which, now that I think of it, is exactly the same law enforcement set-up as Mayberry. The sheriff would often just drop by houses on his route and talk, true community policing long before the term existed. Oconee State Bank opened up around the time we arrived, the first local bank since The Great Depression (Daddy and Mother were founding stockholders). You could buy crackers and milk at the store in Oconee, but if you wanted luxury items, like toilet paper, you had to go to Athens. The county cannery (near where OCAF is today) was a popular meeting spot. High school athletics and church events comprised the majority of our social calendars. We all observed the rules of rural etiquette. For example, when visiting friends you never knocked on doors in the country. You pulled your car up into the yard and honked the horn, giving your friends who lived there time to ready themselves for company, which is rural-speak for putting on clothes. Church revivals in August were the social highlights of the year. Our favorite example of how it was back then has to be when the high school principal would summon us kids to lunch over the PA system with, "Will all the Ag boys come to the cafeteria and set up tables? It's time to feed."

We don't mean to imply that Oconee life was trying. It was great. There was a true sense of community, actually multiple small communities like Farmington and Bishop. Food was fresh and plentiful. Meat was straight off the cow. We all enjoyed the summer blackberries, pears, and figs, all fresh off the vines and trees. The Sunday afternoon double-headers between different churches' softball teams were intense, but played with a spirit of fun. The preacher would rotate his Sunday dinners among the parishioners' families. Neighbors were tight-knit and friendly, and so often related that you were afraid to gossip about anyone, not being sure that you wouldn't inadvertently insult somebody's cousin. Therefore, everyone was polite.

Our moving to Oconee County was a BIG DEAL. We were a big family. We were from Florida. We were successful. We'd bought two whole farms. We even incorporated a little bit of Florida into northeast Georgia, using plaster as a building material instead of the more common sheet rock. Daddy always said one of his happiest times was attending Billy and Bobby's ballgames in high school.

Athens is the big city…at least in relation to life in Oconee County. Where do farm folks go for a night on the town, a trip to the movies, or a date at a nice restaurant? The big city. Though it was only six miles down the road, Athens was an entirely different world. There were all kinds of different restaurants. There were students who'd been born on the other side of the world. There were three movie theaters which we'd take turns visiting on Saturdays (The Palace, The Georgian, and the theaters at Beechwood Shopping Center). It's not Manhattan, but everything's relative in this life.

With new surroundings came new ideas. We switched to raising Angus Beef when we moved to northeast Georgia. Angus was gaining popularity across the country and the world, with its marbling and savory flavor. We bought seed and stock from the Experiment Station just across the road. It wasn't always an easy transition, but we Bishops are survivors.

Kay and Gene, now a married couple, moved into the little, old white house on the Crowley farm. We had to debate where to build what was to become our new home. We settled on the final location to accommodate Mother's wishes. She wanted a great view and didn't want that view to just be of trees. If we're being honest, she didn't want to have to rake leaves, but her wish to create a beautiful view has paid off. Stand on the land and look out over the pastures and slightly rolling hills sometime. It's hard to imagine that there's a more beautiful place on Earth.

The hurdles that America has sometimes placed on farmers, cattle ranchers and dairymen can seem too high to jump. After buying the land, we were compensated on a PPA (price per acre) basis by the USDA, as a part of their conservation agenda. Of course, we also had to find and organize all of the necessities of cattle life, the major prerequisite being water. Luckily, the Bishop family had landed in Aqua-La. The Farm produced six high-quality wells. There's so much water that we still fill the Shamrock swimming pool with our water. The land was amply prepared for our lifestyle. In fact, some experts now predict that Georgia will

replace California as America's premier source of fruit and vegetable production in the near future. At least some of that predic-
tion is based on water. California is running out of it. Southern
Piedmont Georgia isn't.

We were also swimming against the tide of agricultural
trends. In the 1960's cattle wasn't considered a "cash crop." Even
cotton, once widely regarded as King of The South, saw its production decline in the 60's. Chicken houses were all the rage.
Even city folk would put up a chicken house or two on their land
in the country as a way to supplement their incomes. Those long
white A-frame structures could house hundreds of chickens.

With the move our world got smaller. We had stepped
into a county in need of so many of the aspects of community life that we had taken for granted back in Florida. The high
school didn't even have a football team. The gymnasium where
we played basketball had rickety, old wooden bleachers and was
heated by a pot-bellied stove. It was a WPA (Works Progress
Administration, an FDR New Deal project) building. There was
no chorus, no band, no student council, and no yearbook to
document the accomplishments of local students, but there were
basketball games. When Billy was playing basketball he wore his
contacts, which were forever falling out of his eyes. When Billy
would lose a contact during a high school game, the referee would
call a time out and everyone, the home team and the visiting
players, would drop to their knees on the hard wood and help him
find his contact lens. That was Oconee County in those days. The

boys were a little disappointed in not getting to attend high school where their parents had, especially since athletics up here weren't as established as what we'd known in Florida.

The pace of life was much slower. The local flavor of small town America was on full display here. We met our cousins, Ralph Green's children, Marvin and Celestia (what a name!) and became fast friends with them. Children stayed out of school to pick cotton in September. The school was tiny, with only around fifty kids in each grade. Oconee was the tortoise to Daytona's hare. It wasn't easy to adjust to the pure rural life, but at least that meant that the rules were less strict. You could legally drive to school at age fifteen, no license required. You could hunt and no one would bat an eye at the gun shots.

It will likely come as no surprise, but Billy once got paddled by one of his teachers with a miniature canoe paddle, just one of the many strange items people have used to discipline him over the years. Billy's History and Government teacher, a squat, but stocky, muscular Navy veteran and strict disciplinarian was teaching one day when he caught Billy breaking the rules. "Are you chewing gum in my class, Billy Bishop?" A fellow student was also simultaneously busted for gum chewing at that time. After making them spit out the gum, the teacher offered Billy and his classmate their choice of one of two punishment options: either copy the entire United States Constitution out ten times or accept five "licks" from the paddle. The paddle in this case was small, but still incredibly scary-looking! The man administering the "justice" was a strong Navy veteran. Most kids would've chosen the Constitutional option. Billy's classmate did. However, Billy Bishop was never "most kids." Always a little brash, a little daring, Billy chose the paddlin'. As his classmate copied America's founding government document, the teacher laid down the law. "Alright, I will inflict punishment two weeks from today." Billy hoped that he'd forget about it in the intervening weeks, but he wasn't so lucky. The teacher paddled Billy five times…on his rear. According to Billy, "I really thought he'd forgotten about me. By the third smack I was ready to change my mind and do the Constitution, and I tried to raise my hand and opt out, but by that time I'd pretty much lost all feeling back there. So, I let him finish." Discipline was enforced more harshly then, and Billy, being Billy, received more than most.

Athletics have always been a part of our story. Bobby even met his future wife at basketball practice. She was on the girls' team. He was on the boys'. He first saw her when he was going into the gym and she was coming out of it, right next to the old pot-bellied stove. Their meeting fits with the theme of the family story perfectly.

As the pace of life slowed, so did the pace of work. Cattle operations are a different beast from dairies. Billy and Bobby planted Bermuda grass for our 100 or so cows to graze on in their new home. We put up fences. We kept close watch on the stock. We managed to make money and not have every single solitary

1963 Oconee County High School. Bobby #21 Billy #4

minute preplanned for us years in advance.

The 60's changed us in another major way. It was the decade that heralded the changing of the guard in the family. Time passes. There's nothing we can do to stop it. This was the decade that saw the stewardship of the Bishop family change hands, from one generation to the next. We siblings took on more and more of the bigger picture tasks that our parents had once done. We became the "adults." Billy and Bobby were still in school at the start of the 60's. Billy graduated high school in 1963, Bobby a year later in 1964. Kay and Gene both studied at UGA (Masters in Counseling and a B.S. in Business Administration, respectively). Kay was also teaching a combination third & fourth grade class herself. Radford was studying at FSU. His life was in Florida. Our lives were up here. Our parents lives were somewhere in between.

Our mother had moved up with us to Georgia physically, but her spirit was still in Florida. Bobby says it poetically, "Once you get sand in your shoes, you can't get it out." Mother never really took to the area, experiencing health problems almost as soon as we arrived. Her mother Eva died in September of 1962, dealing her, and all of us, a blow. Daddy's mother, Big Momma, died just a year later, in 1963. The death of your mother leaves you rudderless in a stormy sea. We lost both of our grandmothers in a two-year span. It wasn't only Eva Summerlin's demise that made Mother's heart move back to Florida. At Holly Hill, Mother had had a regimen. Up in Oconee County, she was frankly a little bored. She even took to ironing our clothes every day, something she'd never done before, in order to feel productive. In the middle of the 60's, from 64-68, our parents lived half of the time in Georgia and half in Florida. We soldiered on up in the Southern Piedmont.

Daddy and Mother on a cruise

THE SEVENTIES

Mother and Daddy eventually made a permanent move to Florida around 1970. They simply moved back into the home on Flomich which we had left ten years earlier. Around 1974, they built a new home on the back part of the dairy property, next to the Riviera Golf Course. It was a pleasant 3 bedroom home with lots of Florida-style screened in porches, lots of shrubs and great oak trees, making it a very comfortable and agreeable home for them in their "golden years."

The 70's were years of travel for Mother and Daddy. They explored the country and the world in ways they previously couldn't have, taking trips with the Florida Farm Bureau to many domestic destinations, such as Maine, Ohio, Niagara Falls, Texas, and all over the farming states of the Midwest. Daddy loved to study different farm and dairy methods on his travels. They also took trips with Alan West, a Baptist pastor and Mother's cousin, trips to Israel, Europe, Asia and two 21-day trips around the world, stopping in such exotic locales as Katmandu, Nepal, Singapore, Hong Kong, Rome, Switzerland, Hawaii, London, and all points in between.

They managed to pack a lot of travel into the 70's and 80's, always bringing gifts back to all of us when they returned: watches from Switzerland, figurines from Thailand, and carvings from the Orient, to name just a few.

There were pictures, pictures, and more pictures. Mostly slides, hundreds of them, enough to fill multiple carousels. One day we may break out the slides and have a world tour!

Kathleen at Bishop's Glen for Harrell and Radford's memorial

THE EIGHTIES

In 1983, Radford made a deal with Daddy for the 11th Street dairy property, planning on turning the land into a luxurious retirement/nursing home facility. As a lobbyist in the Florida legislature for the Retirement Home Association, he was familiar with the needs of the elderly. He had brought a plan for 20 acres of the original dairy land, the land that Thad and Mozelle, Daddy's parents, had purchased in the 30's.

Thad and Mozelle had begun operating a dairy on this property in the 1930's and, when Thad died unexpectedly in 1941, Daddy continued to run the dairy with his mother until he branched out and started his own dairy on Flomich around 1949. Big Momma, as we called her, sold the dairy in the early 1950's, but kept the land and buildings.

Radford's arrangement with Daddy was to buy the property for a set price. Radford would later increase the price when the development company he set up got involved. He even took in a partner who had built similar facilities. They cut out 5 acres at the

H. Radford Bishop

Bishop's Glen

corner of 11th Street and Canal Road (later renamed Nova Rd.) to sell for a small strip mall shopping center. Daddy made this deal with Radford separate from the rest of us.

He proceeded with the project, named Bishop's Glen. It was a well-constructed, well-maintained facility, which has sold

Groundbreaking for Bishop's Glen

several times, but continues to serve the needs of senior citizens, from independent living to full-on nursing home facilities. Eventually, the project was completed, and Radford sold his interest in Bishop's Glen, the shopping center, and about 20 duplexes he had built on land he received from Big Momma's estate. After this sale, Daddy and Mother intended on living at Bishop's Glen, and making use of the amenities the facility had to offer. They enjoyed the amenities, but never moved to Bishop's Glen.

Our parents' 50th Wedding Anniversary on September 6, 1985 was a big bash. Their anniversary was on the same day as

Harrell and Kathleen's 50th wedding anniversary 1985

Daddy's birthday, so that day was made even more special. Fifty years! By today's standards, that's an almost a biblical marital length. Coming just two years after their 50th high school re-union, Mother and Daddy celebrated some important milestones in the 1980's. Their anniversary party was held at "The Case-ments" in Ormond Beach, a nearby resort area with grand, classic 1920's-style architecture and a feeling of opulence not usually found in north Florida. "The Casements" was originally the Florida residence of famed industrialist, John D. Rockefeller.

As it turned out, Radford moved to Highlands, North Carolina and started an antique business he called The Swan House. He also bought and sold several homes in the Highlands area. Mother and Daddy also did not end up where they'd planned. They moved to Watkinsville around 1994, when Daddy's health had declined significantly, so that we all could help with his care. The true life-cycle of a family consists of one generation birthing and caring for the younger generation, and years later reversing roles, so that the younger generation can care for the older one at the last stage of their life-cycle with love, devotion, and attention. From beginning to end, to beginning to end!

In the 1980's, while the world suffered through the tail end of the Cold War, Daddy had a number of true scares. Due to cancer, a portion of one of his lungs had to be removed. That's never an easy situation, though he did manage it with his usual determination. His health and new semi-retired lifestyle took him and Mother back and forth between Florida and Oconee County often.

Once, a little later in that same decade, Daddy was literally run over by our tractor. He had been out in the field, working on the tractor, doing what he had done for years, and had "parked" it in neutral while stepping off to do something else, when he noticed that the tractor was starting to roll down the hill. Instinctively, Daddy leapt on top of the tractor, trying to stop its descent. He fell off, getting run over by the gigantic back tractor tire in the process. Harrell Bishop had always been a tough sort, a true man's man, with a barrel chest and a muscular frame, but his aging body plus the weight of the gigantic tractor almost did him in. Had he not "bowed up" and instinctively flexed his muscles in that split second, he would've almost surely died that instant. We later learned that Mother thought she was going to lose him that day, sitting with his drooping head and limp body in her lap. She cradled his head and cried. However, Daddy recovered, eventually losing a gall bladder, but not his life. It was touch-and-go for a while there, but he survived.

THE NINETIES

After a series of accidents and setbacks, Mother knew that it was "that time." Harrell was never going to willingly give up the role he had perfected over so many years. For a number of years, she had had to "bring his world closer to where she was" in order to ensure that Daddy would keep on living. He still had much to live for, and she knew it. Their world in Daytona Beach and Holly Hill had changed so much from the time they'd first opened their own dairy they could barely recognize the land anymore. The same idea held true for their lifestyle. The golf course which abutted their land had been hearing complaints from some of their golfers that an elderly man had been walking around in his briefs outside of his house, and showering outside, while they were trying to line up their putts. The golf course was finally forced to build a row of tall Oleander Hedge bushes to obscure the golfers' view of Daddy showering. It's funny to think about, but that was just Daddy doing things the way he'd always done. If people around him wanted to spend their time hitting little white balls with metal clubs instead of milking Guernsey cows, that was their business. He still needed to shower. However, Mother recognized that a change needed to be made, as did we, and so a change was made.

The cottage at Bishop Farms

In 1994, we moved our parents up from Florida and back to Oconee County, Georgia, as their health was declining, especially our father's health. To house them properly, we began to construct a comfortable home. By 1995, once the house was built and furnished, they both moved into the one-story cottage on the top of the hill on the farm, the very same house where we sit and write this book, which we dedicate to their memory. The sliding glass door with its panoramic view of the farm allowed our father to look over his legacy in his final years. People always told him, "Harrell, you're going to die with cow manure on your shoes," but he didn't. He did, however, get to see a working farm, operated by three of his children, in his last days.

They still had many business concerns in Florida. Russ Lathrope, family friend, was able to take care of their Florida holdings after they moved to Georgia.

Though at the end Daddy had to suffer through the common Bishop genetic trait of having bad knees, he still managed to get around pretty well, until the closing chapter of his life when he was, briefly, confined to a wheelchair. In 1998, he did suffer from Alzheimer's Disease at the end, too, but it came in fast, and then he went fast, and relatively peacefully. As that insidious ailment often does, Alzheimer's caused our father to say some things he never would've said before, using let's just say "harsher" language than we were used to hearing.

They settled into a routine up here, always busying themselves with something or another. They attended church with us, always sitting on the lower left-hand side. They took Sunday drives, afternoon jaunts in the country, listening to the radio. They'd outlived all of their Georgia relatives. Our circle of friends and their grandchildren kept them busy and entertained. They were the true hub of the wheel of our family, with us as the sturdy spokes, propping them up and keeping them turning and turning.

Our father, Harrell Bishop, passed away on March 16, 1998, in the bedroom at the back of the house we'd built on the top of the hill at the front of the farm in Oconee County, Georgia, with his beloved wife of almost 63-years, and three of his children and seven of THEIR children nearby. He was able to end his productive time on this Earthly-realm on a farm, with cows, picturesque pasture land, and more farm implements than he could've told us to "Fix" with a hundred yellow crayons. The Lord allowed him to see the future of the Bishop clan spread out in front of him…the passing of a great man, a beloved husband, father, and grandfather, and a faithful follower of Jesus Christ. Amen, Amen!

Grandmother with her grandkids

First Baptist Church Daytona Beach

THE NEXT MILLENNIUM

Our parents' long marriage was one of those couplings of their generation, with a bond forged by time and adversity, strong as a stately Southern oak tree, sure as the sun rises in the East every day. With marriages like that, when one partner passes away, the other usually fades quickly to join him or her. Kathleen Summerlin Bishop, our mother, held on for six more years after Daddy passed.

Always a mover and a doer in life, Mother didn't want to linger in a state of sickness. One week after being diagnosed with "Acute Leukemia," she quietly passed away here in Oconee County, with all of her children and grandchildren at her side. We had all gathered at the cottage on the Farm late in the evening. Robert and Kerry had gone to Savannah to bring Meredith and great-grandchild Katie home to Watkinsville. Mother kept asking, "Were Meredith, Robert and Kerry home yet?" "No, Mother, not yet."

On April 28th, 2004, around 11 PM Robert, Meredith,

Kerry and Katie arrived. "Grandmother, we are here," said Meredith. "Bless you," answered Mother. Within the hour our beloved Mother, devoted to the end to each one of her offspring, faithful to her calling in Jesus Christ, went home, rejoicing all the way, to see her "Babe" and her Lord Jesus. Amen, Amen!

CONTINUING LEGACY

We have created a legacy. There's no better word for it. Family can mean many things, especially in the 21st century, but legacy is something else, something deeper, something one proudly passes down to the next generation in the hope that they will do the same when their time comes. In that spirit, we Bishop siblings have each written a chapter about our nuclear families. We'll go in birth order, meaning that we'll start with Kay:

KAY AND GENE

As the oldest sibling, Kay broke in our parents. It's always this way for first-born kids. The parents are more afraid the first time around, more watchful, less lenient. Our parents learned how to be parents with Kay. Kay and Gene's marriage is a model of how to maintain a loving and stable union.

Kay and Gene met at the First Baptist Church in Daytona Beach, Florida. Gene had moved down from Powellton, West Virginia, to work for his aunts who owned a motel in South Daytona. Kay was teaching 4th grade at Holly Hill Elementary School, after having taught for a year at Fern Park Elementary School near Orlando. Gene was attending Daytona Beach Community College and working at Southeastern Utilities as a bookkeeper.

They started dating after meeting at the annual Sweetheart Banquet at the church. It was a whirlwind relationship that was sealed after Kay returned home from a month-long trip to the Baptist World Alliance Convention in Brazil and a tour of South America. They say that absence makes the heart grow fonder, and so it did with them. A wedding was quickly planned just as the family was in the process of moving to Georgia. On September 3rd, 1960, Kay and Gene were married at the First Baptist Church in Daytona Beach, appropriately where they first met. After a honeymoon to North Carolina and West Virginia, they moved into what had become known as the "Little White House" on the farm in Georgia.

Kay and Gene's Family

Kay enrolled at the University of Georgia in a Master's program in Guidance and Counseling, and Gene enrolled in the Business School at UGA. Both attending school and relying on some small savings to live on, they learned how to make a dollar stretch. Their first major purchase was a chest-deep freezer (which they still use today), a pretty good investment, which was filled with veggies from the garden and meat from the pasture. Kay started teaching grades 3 and 4 at Watkinsville Elementary School. She had some of the same students two years in a row, and still sees many of them today around Oconee. Those were the good old days, when teachers read the Bible each day, had prayers, and led a pledge of allegiance to the American flag. Children knew that, if they didn't behave, they might easily receive a paddlin' from the teacher, and one at home, too.

After graduating from UGA in 1963, Kay and Gene took a month to travel and camp en route to the west coast. It was an exciting time as we ("we" being Gene and I---Who did you think was writing this?) rode across this vast country in our "new" '57 Chevy, enjoying adventures along the way. We kept hungry bears away from our food at Yellowstone. We weathered Dust Bowl-strength wind storms in Oklahoma. We averted disaster with failed brakes in, of all places, Death Valley. And we visited Gene's father in Kelso, Washington. After returning home, Gene started working for the Georgia Revenue Department as an auditor in the Sales Tax Division.

Stephen was born on September 4th, 1965. Our first

house was built that year. Also, Kay was hired as the first full-time Guidance Counselor at Oconee High School. There were a lot of firsts that year...the first school annual (yearbook), the first student council, the first Glee Club. Kay was very busy with new jobs, a new baby, and managing all of the firsts at OCHS.

Gene and Stephen 1965

Kerry was born on June 12, 1968. She attended Billy and Sandy's wedding on June 15, before going home from the hospital. The next years were busy times with two young children, Kay working part-time, and Gene and Kay taking care of things on the farm, as Mother and Daddy had moved back to Florida. During these years, Kay completed her Specialist Degree in Education at UGA, attending classes on weekends and evenings. She didn't have a lot of what they call "free time" in those days, but leisure has never really been our family's main pursuit.

Kerry's 29th Birthday

Both Stephen and Kerry attended and graduated from Oconee County High School, where they were involved in sports, band and FFA. Stephen later went on to the University of Georgia and graduated from the Medical College of Georgia as a Physician's Assistant. Kerry finished two years at Truett-McConnell College in Watkinsville and graduated from Western Carolina University with a degree in Medical Technology. Both children

Stephen and family

ending up in the medical field was completely unexpected by Kay, but what does she know? She was just a high school counselor. It has been both a blessing and a joy to see how God had a plan to use their interests and abilities to serve others. Stephen married Michelle Medley in 1990 and they moved to Augusta, Georgia where he entered the Medical College of Georgia. After gradua-tion and the birth of their son, Connor, they moved to Rock Hill, South Carolina where Stephen began his career in the ER at Pied-mont Hospital. They blessed us with two grandchildren, Connor and Sydney. And, according to Kay, as the saying goes, "If I had known how great grandchildren were I would have started with them first." They are both in college at the time of this writing

(Connor at MTSU and Sydney at Lander University), and our prayer is that they will seek God's will with all of their hearts and be blessed in the way that He will lead them.

In 1982 Kay was instrumental in starting the Truett-Mc-Connell College Off-Campus program at Oconee County High School. From one evening class of 6 students, this program grew over the next 10 years to a full-time college program on the new campus at Bishop Farms.

Kay spent 6 years as the Academic Advisor at Truett-Mc-Connell College, from 1986-2002. These years were especially meaningful to her as she had a part in seeing many students fulfill their desire to complete their college degrees as adults.

Kerry   Kay and Gene

Kay's family with Grandmother and Grandaddy

After 30 years, Gene retired from the State of Georgia Department of Revenue and gave his attention to the farm, his herd of cows, his church and Shamrock Recreation Club. Mr. Gene was known for riding his lawnmower and golf cart all over the area.

He kept things running and moving for many years, until his health got the best of him and he had to "retire" once more in 2012. On February 5, 2016, Gene went home to be with the Lord and so many members of his family. "Well done, thou good and faithful servant," must have been the greeting he received as he entered into heaven.

Watkinsville First Baptist Church played a very important role in both Kay and Gene's lives for 55 years. Gene served as deacon, treasurer, and on building committees, and Kay in the music and mission ministries. Mission trips to Haiti with the church and her parents as well as trips to Romania were life-changing experiences for Kay.

According to Kay, "As I look back over my life through the writing of this book, I see how faithful God has been in leading and directing my path. I may not always have been obedient and faithful, but He has been. I look forward to the day when I see the One who gave His life for me so that I may live with Him eternally."

Radford and family

RADFORD
(H. RADFORD BISHOP II)

Written by his children

Radford Bishop was our older brother. Everyone loved Radford. He was a social animal, always leading a pack of friends around. As an adult, he used his impressive social skills professionally running political campaigns and as a lobbyist, beginning in Florida's capital city, Tallahassee, and later throughout the Southeast and Washington D.C. When we were little, Radford was just our smart, cool and curious brother.

Radford grew up attending the First Baptist Church and school in Daytona Beach. In grade school, he was active in both church and school. He often provided fond recollections of his activities in Sunday school, summer camps, and in raising cows for competitions.

Radford was a popular kid. He loved people and people loved him. Even when he was only in high school, we could see the beginnings of his life in politics. Radford particularly enjoyed his days at Mainland Senior High. He was active with his class leadership and had many good friends. He was particularly

Radford, Lauren, and Blair

involved with the Wheel Club, The Rotary Club's high school
service club, where he was President in his senior year and elected

to the International Board of Directors. In this, he was proud to earn the opportunity to be a delegate at their International Conference in Washington D.C. in 1957.

Radford was many things. He was not, however, a natural dairyman. We remember when Radford learned in high school about the psychologist, Ivan Pavlov, and his famous "conditioned reaction" experiment with his dogs (where Pavlov paired a bell with the feeding time for his dogs, and soon discovered that the dogs were salivating at just the sound of the bell). Radford, always one to experiment, tried to incorporate his newfound knowledge into the dairy regiment. As the sibling in charge of bringing the calves in from the pasture, Radford thought that he'd hit a big spoon on the bottom of a cooking pot as he was herding them inside for their feeding. He figured that soon enough the cows would come at just the sound of the banging spoon. Of course, calves like to graze and they never learned to respond to Radford's homemade gong.

Radford graduated from Mainland Senior High in 1958. In the fall of that same year, he began his studies at Florida State University in Tallahassee, Florida. At FSU, Radford was involved in student politics and earned a B.S. degree in Public Administration in 1963.

During Radford's college years, Fred Karl, a lawyer from Daytona Beach, served in the Florida House of Representatives, and Radford spent many hours helping out in his office. These were the days before House members had professional staff.

About the time Radford graduated, Karl was running for governor and Radford went to work for the campaign, serving as coordinator for North Florida. Karl was not elected. Radford went to work as Assistant to the City Manager of Ormond Beach, Florida, and lived at 230 Daytona Avenue, Holly Hill, in the house his father had built for his young family, and where Radford and Kay had spent many of their growing-up years.

In 1964, Radford married Judy Wheeler, a language arts teacher at Ormond Beach Junior High. In 1965, their first daughter, Lauren Kay, was born, and another daughter, Blair Marie, came into the world in 1966. In 1968, the family moved together to Tallahassee in order for Radford to attend graduate school at Florida State University. That was the same year Karl was elected to the Florida Senate. Since he had served in the House, Karl was appointed chairman of a Special Select Committee on Consumer Finance, and hired Radford to be his staff director. In the next biennium, Karl was made chairman of the Senate Commerce Committee, and again hired Radford to be his staff director. Judy and Radford were divorced in 1974.

In retrospect, Radford's path in life was obvious from his early days. He was always a politician, even in high school, so it wasn't surprising that he wound up working as a lobbyist in Tallahassee. After starting his professional life as a city planner, Radford quickly moved into the world of Florida politics. It was where he belonged. Over the years, Radford lobbied for various organizations, including the senior citizens, and their assisted living homes, like the one he built on the dairy land where his family began farming in Florida. But, our Radford was never one to just do one thing at a time. He was always wheeling and dealing, trying new things over the years: managing properties, opening and operating a store on Peachtree Street in Atlanta, operating a crystal and cut glass store on Preston Street, and overseeing The Swan House, his antique business in Highlands, North Carolina. He wound up moving to Highlands in his later years.

Radford always loved finding and restoring old things. Even as a young boy, he often came home on his bike, his body hidden by the tower of finds he balanced on the way home. He furnished his house with furniture and objects he acquired from auctions and nearly-new stores, one of his favorites being located on Second Avenue in Daytona. Judy's favorite "find" was a round oak table he bought at an auction one night with Gene Strickland. Gene had a station wagon and Radford liked to go to auctions with him so that he could take large things home afterwards. The table had two coats of paint and had been left out in the weather for a long time. He scraped the outside layer off, Strip-Eased the next, and refinished the bare wood so that now it is a family treasure.

In Atlanta, Radford turned his hobby into a business for antiques and decorative objects that he bought at estate sales and auctions. He began in the Atlanta Flea Market and later moved onto Peachtree Street in Buckhead. Still later, he moved to Highlands, North Carolina, and opened The Swan House on Main

Radford Highlands, NC

Street.

Radford also carried his hobby of restoring things over
to real estate. He renovated several homes throughout the years.
His daughters always enjoyed visiting him. It was never boring.
"Daddy was always working. He worked his regular job all week,
and then worked long days at his shop or acquiring goods for

his store. When we visited, it was the same, and we would work along beside him. Some kids might complain about working all spring break, but for us he always made work fun!" The by-line of his store was, "The challenge in life is not affording the best, but finding it!" Radford had the ability to quickly scan an auction or thrift shop and find things of value. He knew the furniture history and construction and could tell certain companies and styles and fakes. He developed a specialty in discontinued fine crystal and Depression-ware and had one of the largest collections in the U.S. in the early 1980's. Many collectors would seek him out for help in replacing lost and broken pieces, and he built one of the first matching services in the South.

Generosity and a keen psychological sense of what people want were always Radford's most prominent traits. He was generous to a fault. Radford was the uncle who would show up on your doorstep at Christmas with a big bag of presents for everybody, graciously giving gifts like a skinny Santa Claus. And they were always good gifts. Accompanying his inherent generosity, Radford had exquisite taste, and so his was the hand that guided young mouths to their first taste of fine food, like Godiva chocolate (widely considered the world's best chocolate).

Radford's business acumen was equally legendary. He had a keen ability to read people, to know their hearts. Inside The Swan House, his antique store in Highlands, NC, Radford stocked many random pieces of Americana, like Coca-Cola crates from thirty years before he put them on sale, or genuine railroad

Lauren and Mike's Wedding with Grandmother

Jimmy and Blair's Family

Susanna's High School Graduation

lanterns that had been out of use for decades. If an item didn't sell, Radford bucked the conventional wisdom and, instead of lowering the price, raised it...and it would inevitably sell just a bit down the road. When customers took no interest in an item, Radford would repaint it a different color...and that worked, too. When Billy was driving him to a chemotherapy appointment one day toward the end of his life, Radford let loose another of his business secrets. When someone came into his store and focused in on one particular item, but didn't purchase it, and then returned to scrutinize the same item again, hoping to nudge Radford toward lowering the price, our brother would spring his trap. They would ask for about the same item, and Radford would tell them, "Oh, you just missed it. I sold it just yesterday." The customer would be disappointed, but Radford would promise them that he was about to get some more of that item in stock, in which case the customer would inevitably be willing to pay the original asking price, if not more. The man flat out knew how to sell to people.

In 1989, Radford got sick and moved back to Atlanta. Unfortunately, it was cancer, though we can feel fortunate that our brother Radford at least had a relatively quick death. His battle with cancer lasted over six months and ended with his family at his side, hand in hand, all of them in one place, singing one of his favorite hymns, "To God be the Glory." Passing away at age 48, Radford's was a life cut far too short, but even with only those limited years our brother Radford left a legacy of kindness and love to all who knew him.

BILLY AND SANDY
written by Billy

I was in the middle of my sophomore year at UGA in 1965. I had been fascinated with New York City (really Manhattan) since seeing the movie "West Side Story" in the early 1960's, and then visiting the city for my Senior Class Trip in June of 1963.

The World's Fair was to open in New York in 1965 and run through 1966. The Fair was massive and everyone said that it would take several days to really see it all. Although I didn't think happiness was seeing Watkinsville in the rear view mirror, I did believe there was more to "it all" than barbecues at Harris Shoals Park on Saturday afternoons.

During the winter months, I had been a regular visitor to the Summer Placement Office at UGA. I first tried to get a job as an NBC Paige on "The Tonight Show." That failed and I quickly applied for a job at the Fair itself, but all of those jobs were taken.

As it turned out, the best I could find was as a camp counselor with the Central New Jersey YMCA's summer camp in the Pocono Mountains of Pennsylvania. Although my idea of camping out was turning off the air conditioner and raising the

Sandy, Scott, and Billy Bishop

bedroom window, I figured that I could stand just about anything for 10 or 12 weeks. The means to an end was what was important.

My closest friend had agreed to go with me, and I immediately sent my signed contract to the Camp Director. After several weeks, he contacted me to say that my friend had not sent his contract to them. I called right away to see what the problem was. My friend, after some hemming-and-hawing, relayed to me that he was going to summer school and had a job counting the number of bumble bees on rows of cotton.

I was not only mad, but very apprehensive, about venturing 800 miles into Yankee territory by myself. So, to get my mind off it, I went to Daytona Beach with some friends.

Of course, my mother was aware of what was going on, and decided to take matters into her own hands. She ran into the mother of one of my high school classmates at the grocery store and discovered that her son was looking for a summer job. Nuff said! Mama called the Camp Director and told him that she had found a replacement for my friend who had backed out. Since time was quickly running out, he said to bring the friend, and we would complete the paperwork when we arrived at the camp.

David and I set out on our trek on a Saturday morning in a 1956 Buick station wagon (a family pass-down), arriving in Washington DC around midnight. We drove around the city for several hours before heading to Baltimore on the Washington-Baltimore Turnpike. We "gave outta gas" about halfway to Baltimore. I quickly realized that the gas gauge was reading a quarter of a tank, so I simply drove off-route onto the wooded grassy median separating the north & southbound lanes. We pulled out our sleeping bags, crawled under the car (in case it rained) and went to sleep.

The next morning I was awakened by someone tapping on my feet. It was a Maryland State Trooper with his "Billy Stick."

"You guys can't camp out on the Parkway!"

I assured him that it was a desperation move, as we had given out of gas. After a short lecture, he took me to get some gasoline, and we were on our way, now carrying some spare gas in a can just in case something like this happened again.

We made it to the camp – Camp Speers for Girls & Camp Speers for Boys – Dingmans's Ferry, Pennsylvania late on a Sunday afternoon. After a quick review of the camp, we immediately began to plot our escape. This place looked bad. A dirt basketball court, primitive cabins, outhouses, the list goes on…

Sunday supper, with only the boys' staff, featured ravioli, a dish which I'd never heard of, much less eaten. Things were so bad that we planned on leaving in the middle of the following night. And then something unexpected happened. At supper the next night, the girls' staff joined us for a meal. AH, HA!!! Some of these girls looked pretty good, so we decided to stay another day. At supper the next night, a new girls' staff member was introduced, and I won't say that it was love at first sight, but I definitely liked what I saw…a lot! Beautiful, big, round blue eyes, long brown hair, a great tan…it all started right then and there.

After several days, I was able to get a date with Sandy (camp name). The only place close enough to the camp to take a date was a local Pocono Mountain Bar that had a connected room where all the camp staffs in the area could meet and eat pizza.

After going a couple of miles on the four- or five-mile trip, the fuel tank reared its ugly head, and I had to stop the car in the middle of the dirt road. I announced that "I just gave outta gas," and began to climb out of the car to get the spare gas can in the back of the station wagon.

Now switch to the mind of Sandy – A Jersey girl! She's thinking (she told me about this months later), What is this guy up to?? He's announced that he has just "passed wind" and now what is he going to do…go into the woods to relieve himself??? I also learned that later that evening, back at the Girls' Camp, she told fellow female staffers that she had just had a date with Gomer Pyle!!!

I did get to the World's Fair a few times, and it turned out to be an enjoyable summer of camping out, canoe trips, and going to the Jersey Shore. I wanted to bring my new "girlfriend" to Georgia to meet my family, but we both had to return to our colleges. A friend and I made several trips to Pennsylvania to visit Sandy at West Chester State College and to New Jersey to spend Thanksgiving with her family, and we also took a trip to NYC.

In Christmas of 1965 Sandy finally came to Georgia. My mom introduced her as "Billy's little friend from the North" and added, "She's a Yankee from New Jersey." Sandy had a very tough time adjusting! The language, the food and the culture were very different. We both returned to Camp Speers the following summer and this summer romance continued to blossom with visits back and forth around school and holidays.

There was a marriage proposal in 1967 and a wedding on June 15, 1968. After graduate school – Billy at the University of South Carolina and Sandy at the University of Georgia – and then army service, gymnastics coaching and judging, teaching swimming and fitness at the YWCO and elementary school physical education, we moved back to Watkinsville where we built our home. Billy developed Killarney West and built Shamrock pool and Sandy continued teaching swimming lessons and coaching gymnastics. She is still teaching swimming, water aerobics and

Billy Bishop and family

Ken and Greer Wells family

judging gymnastics.

In 1976 Kathleen Greer Bishop (named after her grand-mother) arrived, and three years later William Scott Bishop, a 10 pound, 2 ounce baby boy, completed the family. The next several years were filled with church activities, football, baseball, basketball, gymnastics, swimming and diving, and family and friends. Eventually, Greer and Scott went off to college. Greer went to

Scott and Shanna Bishop

Eliza and Stella Bishop

Scott Bishop and family

Billy and Sandy Wedding 1968

Young Harris on an academic and athletic scholarship to play softball. She received the Luke Rushton Scholar-Athlete Award in 1996-97. After transferring to UGA, Greer completed her Master's degree in Athletic Training & Science Education. While she was finishing her service hours for her degree, she spent some time at the Morris Center with a young man as her supervisor – Ken Wells. Within a few years they would become husband and wife. They built a home in the Village at Dove Creek and began their family. Karlee arrived in 2004 and Kendall in 2007. After surprising and frightening en utero surgery at the Children's Hospital of Philadelphia, the miracle twins Kourtney and Kamryn were born in 2008.

Billy and Sandy dating

Billy, Sandy, Greer, and Scott at Daytona Speedway

Scott went to Piedmont to play basketball. After two years, he transferred to Georgia College and graduated in May 2003 with a BS in Business. After graduation and finding a job, Scott bought a house in Watkinsville.

Scott and Shanna Burd met at Georgia College through mutual friends in 2003. Shanna graduated in May 2004 with a BS in Exercise Science. They dated for many years before getting engaged in December 2007. In August 2008, they were wed on Navarre Beach, Florida, in celebration with their family and friends. After college, Scott went to work for Zaxby's Franchising LLC and has been there for 13 years. He is the Operational Design and Improvement Manager for Zaxby's. Shanna worked at the Hallmark Store for 5 years until they closed the store. A few weeks later, on Easter morning, Eliza Rhee was born, on March 31, 2013. Sixteen months later Stella Raee was born, on August 9, 2014. Currently Shanna is a stay-at-home mother of two very active toddlers. Scott and Shanna are both active in sports within the community and church. Scott plays basketball and softball, and Shanna plays tennis and softball. They make a great doubles team! Both are active members of Watkinsville First Baptist Church and love their friends within their church family.

Billy and Sandy are thrilled to have seven beautiful grandkids, all girls (with Addee Alissa arriving in Feb. 19, 2018):

Karlee Wells – the gymnast

Kendall Wells – the softball player, basketball player & swimmer

Kourtney & Kamryn Wells – the horseback riders & swimmers

Kourtney – the basketball player, runner & softball player

Kamryn – the guitar player & swimmer

Eliza & Stella – excitedly waiting to see what activities/sports they will choose

WILLIAM THADDAEUS BISHOP

March 1, 1945 – Born -- Daytona Beach, Florida

1952-53 -- North Ridgewood School

1954-56 -- Holly Hill Elementary

1957-59 -- Central Junior High

1963 -- Graduates from Oconee County High School

June 15, 1968 -- Marries

August 1968 -- Graduates from UGA (University of Georgia)

August 1968 -- Commissioned as Lieutenant in US Army Reserve

1968-70 -- Graduate School -- USC (M.A. in Geography)

July 1970 -- Officer Basic School -- Ft. Eustace, Virginia

1972 -- Masters of Transportation -- USC

1972 -- Consulting Planner -- Wilbur Smith & Associates

1973 -- Land Developer and homebuilder -- Bishop Development
Properties – Cattle farmer

1975-80 -- Coroner of Oconee County

1976 -- Kathleen Greer Bishop born

1979 -- William Scott Bishop born

April 2001 -- Greer marries Ken Wells

February 25, 2004 -- Karlee Grace Wells born

May 1, 2007 -- Kendall Leigh Wells born

August 2008 -- Scott marries Shanna Burd

October 17, 2008 -- Kourtney Summerlin Wells and Kamryn Dailey Wells born (each named after their great-grandmothers)

March 31, 2013 -- Eliza Rhee Bishop born

August 9, 2014 -- Stella Raee Bishop born

February 19, 2018 – Addee Alissa Bishop born

MARILYN "SANDY" BISHOP

May 28, 1945 -- Born in Long Branch, New Jersey

1950-59 -- Attends Oceanport Elementary School

1959-63 -- Attends Long Branch High School

1963-66 -- Waterfront Director, Camp Speers

1968 – Graduates with B.S. in Health, Physical Education, Recreation West Chester State, PA

June 15, 1968 -- Marries WT Bishop, moved to Watkinsville, GA

1968 -- Summer Camp Director, Memorial Park, Athens, GA

1970 -- Earns Masters Degree in Health Education, UGA

1971 -- Teaches P.E. in Columbia, SC

1971 -- Health and Fitness Director, YMCA, Columbia, SC

1971 -- Begins to coach Women's Gymnastics and became gymnastics judge

1971-Present -- Teaches swimming lessons

1971-73 -- Teaches exercise segment on "Today" in Carolina TV station

1971-73 -- Does a live segment on children's gymnastics, "Mr. Knowsit" TV show

1973 -- Moves back to GA, coached gymnastics at Athens Recreation Department

1974-Present -- Serves on ACTS board

1977 -- Owner and coach, Classic City Gymnastics Club

1985 -- Works as Teacher's Aide, Oconee County schools, Special Education

1995 -- Adjunct faculty, Truett-McConnell College

1995 -- Teaches Senior Stretch class, OCRD

1997-Present -- Taught/teaching water aerobics

1998 -- Adjunct faculty, Gainesville College

Bob and Mary

Bobby and Mary Lou's family

BOBBY AND MARY LOU

written, appropriately enough, by Bobby

My first recollection of seeing Mary Lou Pritchett was on a fall afternoon in 1961 at the Watkinsville gym. I was going into the gym for varsity basketball practice and met this cute, curly-headed blond girl coming out the same door. I didn't know her name, but I was obviously interested in knowing who she was. Who wouldn't be? Some four days later I found out that she was in the 8th grade and had classes on the same hall as the 10th graders. As the story goes, it was all over, and the rest became the history of our love story.

Our high school romance was typical of the age: up and down, little spats, writing notes to each other in class, pulling friends into our drama, and always making up! We both played varsity basketball and would ride the school bus to out-of-town games. Meeting out front of the courthouse, getting a Cherry Coke at Mr. Jim Booth's store, eyeing each other across the aisle in the late-night post-game ride back home. Of course, I was the upperclassman, by two grades. It was a miracle that Mary Lou's mom and dad would let their 9th grade daughter go to the 1963 Junior/Senior Class Prom, but I had carefully "snowed" them with my charm and my boy-from-Florida stories. To my knowledge we still hold the record at OCHS for attending four consecutive Jr./Sr. Proms with the same date (my two proms and then Mary Lou's two proms).

I graduated high school in 1964 in a class of 51 seniors. I was elected class Vice President. I enjoyed the FFA (Future Farmers of America) field trips to different farms. The boar hog cuttings were always a challenge. Taking cows to the auction barn, baling hay and planting Coastal Bermuda hay sprigs were all feats of hard work, but we survived. In fact, high school was fun and exciting, even factoring in the adjustment from the more urban Florida to the rural Oconee setting. Helping dad with the family cattle farm was hard work, but never overbearing. In fact, it was comforting for us kids to see our parents enjoy the new, slower pace of life. Mom and dad were able to attend all of our basketball games, something that never could have happened in Florida. We were even able to take family vacations together, mainly to the big house in Franklin, North Carolina.

After high school, I was accepted at UGA that very summer quarter of 1964. It was hard and I wasn't used to that. My first college class was English 101, taught by a retired Army officer with a raging "Napoleon complex." He chewed my sentence structure up and spit it out all over me, in front of the whole class. However, I managed to survive that first trying summer, and started off my college career as an Animal Husbandry major (seeing myself as a dairyman or cattleman for life, for obvious reasons). One-and-a-half short years later, I finally realized that I didn't want to milk cows for the rest of my life, and changed majors to Agricultural Engineering, the only engineering major offered at UGA at the time. I was somewhat interested in math and engineering-type projects and I liked the idea of designing tools to help other people, people who were not me, milk the cows. That being said, if it weren't for my major professor, Dr. Wilbur Ratterree, I would never have graduated with an Ag Engineering degree.

In my early college years, Mary Lou was still in high school. As it often does, this arrangement led to quite a few break-ups and make-ups. I believe the fact that we were both Christians and both strived to live up to that calling was a large part of the reason we were able to work through our differences and our tough times.

I asked Mary Lou for her hand in marriage on New Year's Eve night in 1967, in the parking lot of Poplar Springs Baptist Church on Colham Ferry Rd. She said yes. We were married the following September 7th, 1968. We were both seniors at UGA at the time (she had caught up with me by going straight through her undergraduate BS work in 3 years—in my defense my degree required 115 hours to her 100 hours). She was a much better student than I was, for sure. We were married the same summer that I attended summer basic training at Fort Bragg, North Carolina and she had a summer internship in the Home Economics Department's Home Management House. Both of these were physically and emotionally demanding. We had a wedding to plan and a new life together to begin.

During college I had joined the ROTC program with the Army. These were the Vietnam War years, when the war was going strong. I received a deferment to finish my BS degree and decided to add an MS degree after my 1969 graduation, leading to my receiving a Second Lieutenant commission from the U.S. Army after school. I taught a surveying class and worked on my Master's thesis in Ag. Engineering, while Mary Lou started her MS work in Early Childhood Development. Our first years of marriage were spent living in the basement of my parents' home. My brother Billy and his wife Sandy were also finishing college and living on the main floor of the house. We had little money, and so I worked at the cattle auction barn on Wednesdays and Mary Lou worked part-time as a secretary at the Ivey car dealership. Our graduate programs also paid us each a small stipend. We made ends meet, but just barely.

On January 5, 1971 we packed all of our worldly belongings into the smallest U-Haul trailer available and headed out to Aberdeen Proving Ground, Maryland for two years of active duty Army life. We were both scared, neither of us having left Watkinsville since the Bishop move in 1960. Army life was an adjustment. It was a strange place. We knew no one. I had 11 weeks of Basic Officer Ordnance School, followed by 12 weeks of Basic Mechanical Officer School. As we both look back over those nearly two years of military life, we can now retrospectively see the fun and the growth in our lives that time provided. We were very fortunate to make friends with other Christian couples who lived faithful lives. The threat of being shipped off to Vietnam was always looming over our heads. The Army tried to entice us to add a third year to my duty, offering to send us to Europe for a year. We declined. Fortunately, the Vietnam War was coming to an end and I never had to go. Instead, I was assigned to Yuma Proving Ground in Arizona, a post 25 miles from town in the arid Southwestern desert.

Arizona was a big surprise! We drove from Watkinsville to Yuma, straight through, stopping only at nightfall. When we got to Yuma we saw one main street that intersected with a state road. At that intersection there was a sign that read, "Yuma Proving Ground, US Army, 25 miles out in the desert." OH NO! We drove the 25 miles that came to the fort main entrance that had two artillery guns, six palm trees and brick wall that read, "Welcome, Yuma Proving Ground." There was not a building in sight. We turned in the road and went about one mile and saw the first building, a WWII Quonset hut. We thought for sure we would be spending the next 18 months huddled in a tiny metal building. The signs directed us toward the post entrance, as we drove over several small hills, we topped the last hill which looked over a palm tree-laden oasis. The post was built along the Colorado River, which was the most lush, green Utopia anyone could ever imagine.

I was assigned to the maintenance shop for all the support vehicles on base. The Proving Ground's mission was to test all of the Army vehicles, machinery, aircraft and support supplies in desert conditions. There were 800 military staff and 2500 civilian employed at the base. We had an officer's club, swimming pool, restaurant, bowling-alley, picture show, dental clinic, PX store, almost everything a small town would have.

We water-skied on the Colorado River in January. We went to San Diego, California for weekend visits. We made crafts in the Post craft shop. We had it made! I received my 1st Lieutenant bars while at Yuma. We had vacations to The Grand Canyon, Montana, and Disney Land, making life-long friendships with people whom we still love. We thoroughly enjoyed those months. We bought our first new car, a Datsun 240-Z (1972). I, along with some other guys, joined the Marine Air Station Flying Club. It was located in Yuma. I had a Major in the Marine Flight Group who taught me how to fly a single-engine Cessna Piper Cherokee. I was flying solo within 8 hours of in-flight instruction. We would fly about 5 miles west of Yuma to small WWII air strips to practice our landings and take-offs.

Our time in Yuma provided us many memories. On one momentous flight, I was alone and scheduled to fly to Blythe, California, about 100 miles north of Yuma. Blythe is usually one of the hottest places in America during the summer. I was about 10 minutes into my flight when I realized that the communication radio was not working. That's usually not a big deal, but a pilot does need it to land back at Yuma Airfield, since it had a control tower. Therefore, I turned around and started back to Yuma. The protocol for signaling to the Tower was to fly parallel to the runway about ¼ mile off the runway. As you pass by the Tower, you are to wave your wings up and down to signal that you don't have radio contact. In return, someone in the Tower would either give a flashing light or flag signal in return to indicate that they understood the crisis and would divert all other air traffic. Well, there was no such signal! So I went east of the airstrip and waited for another plane to show up. In about 10 minutes I spotted a small airplane coming in for a landing. I lined up about ¼ mile behind him and followed his plane in for a landing. Once on the ground, I called the Tower to see what was going on. Of course, they said that they never saw me. Needless to say, my flying experiences after that were a lot more cautious.

Then there was the trip Sandy Bishop, my sister-in-law, made to Phoenix to drive back home with Mary Lou. We picked her up at the Phoenix airport and when we turned to go to the tarmac, she asked where our car was. We said there was no car, but that we were riding in a single-engine airplane. For a moment, I wasn't entirely sure if she was going to get in the plane. Yuma was a great time for Mary Lou and I and we wouldn't change a thing. About 20 years later we revisited Yuma Proving Ground with our three children. We were surely blessed for those years and all of the years since then.

We returned to Watkinsville in late 1972. That was where we wanted to settle. Our roots were deep in Oconee County, and we believed that it was a great community to raise a family. Mary was offered a position in UGA's Early Childhood Department, teaching students in the classroom and at the university's preschool teaching lab. I opened a land surveying and engineering company in Watkinsville.

In the 1970's, the region was changing. Oconee County began to build subdivisions and recreational facilities. Our family decided to take a portion of the farm and develop a residential subdivision. Mother and Daddy deeded 90 acres to the Bishop Development Company (Kay, Radford, Billy and I were the Bishop Development Company.). We started this project by cutting off 60 acres for a 44-lot subdivision and a community pool. Unfortunately for us, America dipped into a recession in the mid-70's which drove interest rates up to 18% and virtually shut down residential development for a time.

I was out of work and needed a job. Daddy asked me to come to Holly Hill to determine if the 11th Street Dairy property could be developed into a retirement mobile home park. During the summer of 1974 I spent many days in Holly Hill, creating a design, figuring costs, and compiling plans for a 20-acres mobile home park. When I presented the plan to Daddy, he opted not to pursue the project. I vividly remember the day he told me to "Go home and get a job." At the time I was hurt, but later realized that it was the best advice he ever gave me.

I returned home discouraged, but with resolve to get a job to provide for my family. Soliciting the help of my college department, Agricultural Engineering (Ag.Engineering), I was told that in just a few days a recruiter from the Georgia Environmental Protection Division was coming to UGA.

I went to the recruitment seminar where I met the EPD region manager for the Albany, GA office, Floyd Childs. He encouraged me to put in an application to the State EPD office. I did so, and, on October 16, 1974 I began what would turn into a 31-year career with the EPD.

Over the 31 years with the Georgia Environmental Protection Division, I was given the opportunity to be on the ground floor of a period of time where we cleaned Georgia's streams and lakes and improved the state's air quality. I felt responsible for making my career a benefit to my state and my community. This career gave me the chance to travel throughout Georgia to clean up polluted areas, take steps to prevent damage to our natural resources, and enhance the use of Georgia's abundant wild resources to better serve Georgia and all of America.

In 1975, our first child, Meredith Leigh, was born. We were excited parents, filled with the wonder and joy that comes with being first-time parents. Mary resigned her teaching job at UGA and transitioned to a stay-at-home mom. I took a position with the Environmental Protection Division of the state of Georgia. My office was in Atlanta, and I began an Oconee-to-Atlanta commute which would last for 19 years.

Our next child, Robert Wesley, was born in 1978. He was named Robert after Bob and Wesley after Mary Lou's father. Life was wonderful on the farm, being the parents of two beautiful children. We were very involved in our church. I was a deacon. Mary Lou was the Nursery Coordinator.

Our next child, Jonathan Luke, was born in 1980.

Life continued on its journey to greatness as our children attended the public schools, and we became very involved parents. I coached Little League and Recreation League Basketball. Mary Lou became the band booster president and the P.T.O. president for many terms.

As we look back on these years, we remember them fondly, especially the pride we felt in watching our kids play sports and perform band concerts. Both sons played football, baseball, and basketball. Our daughter, Meredith, was a very gifted writer and musician. She involved herself with the band and creating the yearbook.

Meredith would grow up and attend the University of Georgia, receiving a Bachelor's and a Master's Degree in Social Work.

Robert attended UGA, and then transferred to Piedmont College, where he earned a degree in Business.

Luke received Criminal Justice and Political Science Degrees from Georgia Southern University.

All three children married and settled in our hometown, and have blessed us with grandchildren. Again, we are now experiencing the joy of family as grandparents.

I have been very involved in my retirement years, with construction of a life building and a children's building at Watkinsville First Baptist Church. My brother Billy and I also started a construction and building company called Fifteen Properties.

Mary Lou is enjoying her retirement years spending time with grandchildren and being a friend and mentor for many young women and their families.

Mary Lou and I continue to be blessed to live on the farm in Oconee County.

Watching the next generation of our family come to the farm to enjoy the cattle, to fish in the lake, and to explore the natural world is a joy. All grandparents should be afforded this opportunity.

GEORGE ROBERT "BOBBY" BISHOP

May 29, 1946 -- Born

1952 -- Attends North Ridgewood Elementary School

1953-57 -- Attends Holly Hill Elementary School

1958-59 -- Attends Central Junior High

1964 -- Graduates from Oconee County High School

September 7, 1968 -- Marries Mary Lou Pritchett

June 9, 1969 -- Commissioned as Lieutenant in U.S. Army Reserve

1971-72 -- Serves in United States Army

1972-76 -- Serves in U.S. Army Reserves, completed with rank of Captain

1973-74 -- Works as Oconee County Land Surveyor

December 1974 -- Graduates Masters program at UGA, with an MSAE degree

October 1974-May 2005 -- Employed by the Georgia Department of Natural Resources, E.P.D.

1975 -- Meredith Leigh Bishop born

1978 -- Robert Wesley Bishop born

1980 -- Jonathan Luke Bishop born

June 1991-Present -- Serves on board of directors of Oconee State Bank

July 13, 2001 -- Kathryn Grace Marlowe born

November 20, 2004 -- Luke marries Samantha Pierce

2004-05 -- Serves as Project Manager for Watkinsville First Baptist Church construction of Life Building

2005 -- Retires from the E.P.D.

August 23, 2005 -- John Luke Bishop born

April 2007 -- Samuel Pierce Bishop born

2007-Present -- Serves as Chairman of the Oconee County Tax Equalization Board

2008-2009 -- Serves as Project Manager for Watkinsville First Baptist Church construction of Children's' Building

September 4, 2009 -- Anna Kate Bishop born

November 19, 2011 -- Meredith marries Daniel Marlowe

October 26, 2013 -- Robert marries Julie Brinson

February 27, 2016 -- Leah Rose Marlowe born

2013-2016 -- Founding member of Living Hope Church

December 9, 2017 – McClain Robinson Bishop born

MARY LOU PRITCHETT BISHOP

November 30, 1948 -- Born

1954 -- Attends Bishop Elementary School

1956 -- Attends Watkinsville Elementary School

1966 -- Graduates from Oconee County High School

1968 -- Marries George Robert Bishop

1969 -- Graduates from University of Georgia, with a B.S. degree

1970 -- Graduates Masters program, M.S. in Education and Child + Family Development

1971 -- Serves as instructor at Arizona Western College

1972-77 -- Serves as instructor at UGA, in Child + Family Development department

1975 -- Meredith is born

1978 -- Robert is born

1980 -- Luke is born

1985-92 -- Works as Nursery Director for Watkinsville First Baptist Church

1986-88 -- Works as a Oconee County High School Vocational Long-Term Substitute

1986-88 -- Works at a teacher at First Presbyterian Day School

1998-99 -- Works at University of Georgia Extension

2000-03 -- Serves as adjunct faculty member and Advisor at Tru-ett-McConnell College

2005-08 -- Works as G.E.D. Instructor at Athens Technical College

2013-16 -- Founding member of Living Hope Church, Athens, GA

Bob and Mary with family Bishop

Bob and Mary with granddaughter Leah Rose

Robert, Julie Bishop, and McClain

Luke and Samantha Bishop family

The Magnolia Tree

HERITAGE

It's a little-understood word. Heritage is bigger than tradition, wider than ritual, and deeper than pride. Remembering who you are, your essence, is a lot like the idea of faith. It helps you get through the rough patches in life.

When we moved to Oconee County and bought the Farm, we inevitably had a few offers to buy parcels of it from various local businesses. We dismissed most of them, but we wound up selling a few plots. For example, we sold a piece of land to the First American Bank in 1999, but added the caveat that they not cut down the huge, centurion Magnolia tree next to the road. The bank had planned on uprooting it, but the community loved that tree. It was a local landmark. We knew that we'd be tarred and feathered if we let them tear it down. Also, it's a really beautiful tree. As we were right smack in the middle of this dilemma, we employed a technique that had worked well for the family before and turned a negative into a positive. We contacted arborists and conservationists around the area and helped the bank turn this immovable object into the focus of their venture. They now have brochures about the history of the Magnolia tree available inside the bank. They can tell you the oral history of their construction headache-turned visual centerpiece. Of course, Daddy would be proud. We sold 2 acres and bought a 60-acre farm on McRee Gin Road, south of Watkinsville, a pretty good exchange! This is just one example of a larger family trend.

LEGENDS, HEROES AND TALL TALES

(Unconnected tidbits we wanted to include):

#1
FRAT VERSUS FARM

"Did Billy and Bobby ever get in trouble?"

"Why yes, yes they did."

This is a little anecdote that tells not only what UGA was like when academic giants like Dean Tate roamed the campus, his power supreme, but also what Billy and Bobby were like when they let their mischievous sides take control.

There was a snowstorm in Athens and Oconee that year. It does snow here, but not very often. Florida boys don't know much about snow. Georgia boys know a little more, but unlike, say, boys from Michigan, snow is a rare enough occurrence that its presence tends to bring out a childlike sense of awe and wonder and a burning desire to mess with people.

To set the scene a little, the fraternity boys liked to taunt the country boys and they saw the freak Georgia snowstorm as a perfect opportunity to assert their dominance. Their frat houses were mainly lined up in a row and so, when some of them decided to make a bunch of snowballs and toss them at passing cars, they had a firmly established territory. They were snow-armed and snow-ready.

Billy and Bobby had other ideas. Along with their friend Major, Billy and Bobby turned a simple cattle truck into a mobile snow tank/coolest automotive snow truck south of the Mason-Dixon Line. Filling 55-gallon drums with snow and reinforcing the borders of the back of the truck, the boys created the perfect snow weapon and a means to show the frat boys who really ran things. Using the hay bales at their disposal, the snow-tank was given fortifications behind which the boys could hurl snowballs and feel protected. After a few hours of careful planning, the snow-mobile was ready.

Billy and Bobby purposefully drove the vehicle down to fraternity row, slowed down to a crawl and, as expected, were pelted with snow armaments from the waiting frat boys. Parking their snow-tank, the boys launched a surprise attack, peeking out from behind their fortifications, they leaped up and began snow-barraging the frat boys with snowballs. They balled the ballers and were clearly winning, when some scared frat boy, humbled by his inferiority to Billy and Bobby, called the UGA campus police. Billy wasn't enrolled that semester, but was set to attend UGA the next quarter (this was back in the days of the quarter system), meaning that he thought that he was beyond the reach of the campus police. The fact that the campus cops sided with the frat boys didn't help anything. Feeling understandably disrespected, Billy proceeded to aggravate the situation. Things were getting heated, or as heated as snowballs fight aftermaths get.

That's when Dean Tate showed up. Dean Tate was the legendary Dean of Men, a gigantic man whose imposing size and demeanor loomed large over the school for the better part of the 20th century. With his barrel chest and his little round glasses accentuating his enormous stature, Dean Tate cruised in to put an end to the situation. To put it bluntly, the siblings all agreed on the following, "We don't remember who the president was, but we sure remember Dean Tate." When Tate showed up, he, as he usually did, wanted to clear up the situation without leaving any lasting scars on his students. He had never had a UGA student arrested before, a point of pride for him, but Billy and Bobby were pushing the envelope.

There was squabbling. There was anger and resentment. And there was a lot of snow. As she was in a respectable position of academic authority as the guidance counselor of the Oconee County High School, Dean Tate called Kay to try and settle the affair. She arrived on the scene, and, after a little wrangling and a thirty dollar contribution to the student fund, Dean Tate agreed to let the parties all go their separate ways. No one got arrested, but

Billy did have to cool his heels with the police. They even took his shoes and his belt, to keep him from hanging himself (which would've been historically important, making him the first local snowball-related suicide).

The resentment still simmered, but the heat was turned off for now. The farm boys officially won the battle, but the war was far from over.

#2
MEMORABLE FAMILY VACATIONS

MENU PROBLEMS AT THE PANTHER CREEK CAFÉ
(Tallulah Falls, GA)

Have you ever eaten at a restaurant and had a waiter come back to your table from the kitchen five or six times telling you that "We're out of that today"? We have. The place was called The Panther Creek Café, located in scenic Tallulah Falls, in the north Georgia Appalachian foothills. Judging from our lack of success with the menu at The Panther Creek Café, we'd have probably had an easier time ordering actual panther meat. We'd all place an order. The waiter would write it down, and then toddle back to the kitchen. Then he'd come back after three or four minutes and say, once again, "We don't have it." This little hunger dance went on for about thirty minutes. I think we wound up ordering raw hamburger meat and taking it home to cook burgers. If you're hungry for a memorable, funny experience, we'd recommend it, but if you're hungry for dinner, whatever you do, don't eat at The Panther Creek Café.

SKI TRIP

We took a family ski trip to Vermont one year, the whole family. Some of us were more experienced skiers than others. Two of our, let's just say, "less-seasoned skiers," Sandy and Kerry, wound up getting on the wrong ski lift and ended up at a place where they had two choices: ski one of the dreaded black diamond slopes (the notation for the harder slopes), or build a fire and sleep on the snowy mountaintop for the night. Seriously, what else could you do in this scenario?

Ski lifts move fast, especially when they're depositing skiers at the top of runs. Though it is technically possible to ride a lift down a hill, the set-up of the lifts discourages it, since the whole point is to ski down the hill. Sandy knew she was in trouble when ski lift didn't stop at the top, but shot her out of the seat as it headed downhill! Black diamond runs are known for their moguls (ski-term for large bumps of packed snow). Beginning skiers, like Kerry and Sandy, if they want to avoid moguls, basically have to walk down mountains, inching slowly forward, while wearing the world's longest shoes. It was funny to the two of them, who couldn't stop laughing, but it wasn't funny to Kay in the moment. She was worried and waiting at the bottom of the hill, having sent out the Ski Patrol to look for them. After a few hours of inching forward and down by Kerry and Sandy, a Ski Patrol worker finally found them hugging some mountain trees and asked them jokingly, "Looking for maple syrup, are you?"

WATCH THE WEATHER CHANNEL BEFORE YOU TAKE A CRUISE

Another funny family vacation memory/disaster happened to the Bishops at sea. We took a Caribbean cruise one year, one stormy year, one really stormy year. While we don't recall all of the details, we all vividly remember the dinner plates rolling around the table at every meal, the ship rocking back and forth, as we were trying to feed ourselves, and the ship almost leaving Blair in some port of call.

The weather can turn on a seaman quickly, but on a modern luxury cruise, you do expect a certain level of luxury, or at least an experience more like a hotel and less like an 18th century pirate ship. The brochure can say whatever it wants, but Carnival can't control the weather. It also can't control Blair. Blair is the Bishop whose vivid imagination and almost other-worldly sense of time and space has gotten the family into some tight spots before. One time in Burlington, Vermont, on the way to the airport, Blair wandered off and Sandy spent three hours throwing open shop doors and yelling for her at each and every store, before finally finding her.

On the cruise, though, the tension and drama were magnified when Blair, Jimmy and Meredith didn't show back up at the docked ship on time, the captain was literally about to leave them and shove off. Mary Lou had to stand on "the plank" and physically insert herself as a monkey wrench to stall the captain for time as they wandered leisurely back to the cruise ship. We almost lost them that day, but the Bishop family looks out for each other, and if that winds up making a few sailors mad, so be it.

#3
STRONG WOMEN IN THE FAMILY

We've always had strong women in the family, tough and tenacious females who could handle anything the men could. Our Aunt Doris was a famous sports writer at a time when the industry was completely dominated by men. She was a true pioneer, earning national accolades and carrying on the Bishop family's love of athletics.

Big Momma was a famous entrepreneur. When she died, she'd amassed so much property that she was able to subdivide it into eleven good-sized parcels, to be allotted to members of the family.

Although her humility would keep her from admitting it herself, Kay is a strong woman in her own right. When our parents passed, she took the reins and has kept this family together through sheer force of will.

Sandy and Mary Lou are strong women. Sandy's generous spirit has led her to round up presents for needy Mexican families every Christmas for decades. Mary Lou's calm demeanor and skill set has afforded her the opportunity to be a friend to many young families and to mentor countless young women.

The next generation of Bishop women and the generations to come will likely retain this trait.

#4
NOT CARELESS…JUST DARING

written by Billy

My first vivid memory as a child is being driven home from the beach, wrapped in a wool blanket. Earlier in the day, while on a family outing at the beach, I had darted from the line of parked cars toward the ocean and had been hit by a car and dragged down the beach. Mama told me years later that the car had been driven by a young man from Tennessee. It was totally my fault and, besides having scrape marks and imbedded sand all over my body, I was fine. A small scar on the outside corner of my left eye was the only visible sign of the incident. As near as I can determine, I was four-years-old at the time.

Later that same year (1949), while playing in the backyard (230 Daytona St.), my older brother Radford dropped a concrete block on my face, breaking my nose. The doctor came to the house and, while Daddy held me down, the doctor stuck a stick up my nose, setting the break. Years later I learned this was how doctors fixed boxers' broken noses (my family loved boxing, so it was family tradition).

The next year (1950), while Daddy was attending a Dairy-men's Workshop in Atlanta, I fell out of a tree and broke my right arm. Believe it or not, this was my first X-Ray and first cast.

Things were quiet for the next couple of years, and then in 1952, in the 1st grade at age seven, I darted again (There may be a pattern here.). Radford and I would ride our bicycles the 10 blocks from home to Northridge Wood School every day. Most of the road crossings were residential with relatively light car traffic. However, one intersection, Mason Avenue and Mulberry Lane, was heavily traveled. As we approached the busy intersection that morning, I darted ahead of Radford. I remember his shout-ing, "BILLY!" The next thing I remember is laying in the road and people gathering around me. My mangled bike lay nearby, and I had no idea what was to come! The collision with the car had thrown me into the air and broken my right femur in two. It was a bad break which required four screws and a metal plate to connect the two broken bones. The fact that I was only seven-years-old meant that other medical procedures were needed to assure that no twisting of the femur would occur. I was put into a full-body cast which went from my toes to my upper chest. This left me completely immobile. Someone had to help with all of my basic needs. In other words, it was torture for a seven-year-old boy.

Nonetheless, the family went to our house in North Carolina for a vacation. It was much cooler up in the mountains. We didn't have air conditioning at home in Daytona Beach in those days. It's hard to even describe how hot it was. Think about the beach, then add the lack of air conditioning, and then add a full-body cast to that. By the time of our mountain vacation, I had been in the cast for several months and the healing was progressing slowly. Although the break was internal, I did have two open wounds: one at the pin location and the other a surgical incision. After being in the mountains for about a week, I developed an itching sensation inside my cast. At first it was bearable, but quickly became more intense, and was only relieved by inserting a straightened coat hanger down into the cast and scratching, not the easiest maneuver in the world. Finally, it became so unbearable that we picked up and headed back to Daytona and the hospital.

The emergency room doctor immediately cut open the cast…and the smell was overwhelming. That wasn't even the worst part. My castless body revealed hundreds of what appeared to be maggots on the open wound where the pin had been inserted through my knee. MAGGOTS??? No, they weren't actually maggots, but they were just as bad. They were screw worms. During the 1950's, screw worms were not uncommon and were identical to maggots, except for the horrible fact that they fed only on live flesh. It seemed that a screw worm fly had entered my cast and laid eggs, eggs which hatched into worms, worms that were currently devouring my flesh. Can you imagine? By the later 1950's, the USDA had completely eradicated the screw worm fly by releasing sterile males into the fly population. Sadly, that was a little too late for me. The only aftereffects were two small indentations and scars where the pin had been inserted.

The next two episodes, for lack of a better word, were similar in several ways. In the 4th grade, I crashed my bike in the neighbors' driveway, cracking my elbow. Three months in a cast! The next year, in the very same accursed driveway, I was run over by a homemade Go-Kart, breaking my right forearm. Three more months in a cast! Horrible, but at least there were no flesh-eating worms.

Things quieted down for the next three years. No problems? Largely, but I do remember this being the time when I got multiple cavities from baseball card bubble gum.

Then, in the 8th grade, during a P.E. football game, I got whacked! While running back a kick, one of my best friends tackled me. When I got up, it was obvious that I had broken my wrist (I was getting good at noticing these things). I screamed for the coaches to pull on my arm and put my hand and wrist back in place. Although it was somewhat painful, it didn't swell or discolor. The next morning, I went straight to the hospital. The doctor met us at the Emergency Room and looked at the X-Rays with

Daddy. Then they had a muffled conversation which I couldn't hear. I later learned that they were planning to have an orderly hold me down and have the doctor set the break by pulling and manipulating my arm, thus avoiding a medical procedure. PAIN!!! I have to admit it was over quickly and I don't remember having any lingering pain. Three more months in a cast!

In early 1960, I had barely gotten over the broken wrist when I began to have attacks of abdominal pain, which would last for several hours and result in rather violent vomiting. Mama would always ask me what I had eaten earlier that day and, after telling her she would say, "No wonder you are sick at your stomach." She may have had a point, but this wasn't mere indigestion. One night that spring, after vomiting all night, the doctor came to the house (they still made house calls in those days) and, after a quick examination where the sun don't shine, he said, "Get him to the hospital as quickly as you can. He's got a red hot appendix." No junior high school graduation! No Babe Ruth All-Star Team! No last few weeks with lifelong classmates before moving to Georgia! It was a real bummer. It should be noted that, during this period, my siblings sustained zero injuries. Zero! It was just me, taking one for the team.

I made it through high school with only a couple of sprained ankles from playing basketball. Fast forward to 1995 before I had another injury. Thirty-five years with no major injury. Considering my early history, that's pretty impressive. While working on a small cabin on the farm lake, I fell off the roof, breaking my left calcaneus (heel bone). This was the most painful of all my injuries, and the healing process took over 16 months and included more surgery to remove the hardware initially implanted because the wound would not heal.

The remaining years of the 1990's were uneventful, except for a caterpillar sting that sent me to the Emergency Room posthaste.

Aging had set in, and in the year 2000, while with my Race Team at Daytona, I suffered a mild heart attack, requiring the insertion of two stents. This was followed, in 2010, by two kidney stone attacks, both requiring that the stones be removed with a procedure I really don't want to describe (be happy that I'm not going into details here). And, finally, in 2014, after coming to the point of barely being able to walk, I had to undergo a total knee replacement, where the surgeon removed some metal shards left over from my broken femur in the 1950's. It all came full circle.

#5
HARRELL BISHOP'S BUSINESS SENSE WAS OFF-THE-CHARTS GOOD

Daddy had the unique ability to "see" business opportunities before they happened, almost a sixth sense. He could assess an opportunity in a second at an auction or estimate the future worth of land that was for sale long before others could see it. The Georgia farm was one of Daddy's most profitable investments. In 1958, having already decided that the "days were numbered" for the Holly Hill Dairy Farm, he implemented a well-planned and intricate strategy of shifting from an arduous 24/7 workday life to the more relaxed lifestyle of a beef cattle farmer. When looking for a location in Georgia to set down his family and start up his new dream, Oconee County was an obvious choice: 7 miles away from Athens and UGA, 60 miles east of Atlanta (the largest city in The South), Watkinsville's new high school, a predominantly agricultural area, our ancestral ties to nearby Greene County, and we had Lovern and Bishop extended family in the region. All of the pieces came together to form our perfect landing spot.

The farm was actually two farms, side-by-side, comprising

a total of 410 acres. It was located halfway between the Oconee County Courthouse and the new Oconee County High School, about a mile away from each.

How did we pay for this huge farm? The USDA's "Soil Bank" program was passed by Congress in order to preserve farm soils. The program would pay $5/acre/year to change row crop land into permanent grass cover. Do the math. $100/acre price of land minus Soil Bank payments of $5/acre/year at 200 acres for ten years equals $10,000. That was ¼ the cost of the entire farm. 50 years later the farm's value has reached so high that it comes out to a 700% increase.

Another example of Daddy's ingenuity is the breeding of the dairy herd with an Angus beef bull. This allowed for a ½ milk breed and ½ beef breed, resulting in an excellent herd of broad cows that produced a greater quantity of milk for their offspring.

And we kept repeating this, generation after generation, so that the herd progressed from 50% beef + Angus bull = 75% Angus offspring + Angus bull = 88%, and so on, until, by the fourth generation you have a 91% Angus beef bred herd.

LESSON LEARNED – Realistically assess your present situation. Look for a change to improve your lifestyle and long-term family security. Then execute your well-developed plan at the right time and bathe the whole plan in prayer, asking for God's blessing. Voila! God is good!

#6
A FEW TOTALLY UNCONNECTED BISHOP FACTS

Bobby was born on the beach side. Daytona is a divided town, generally speaking, with the rich people on the beach side, and the poor people on the inland side. Daytona had the standard railroad track class divider, but we took it even further and added a canal. We Bishops were inlanders, but Bobby was born into the world of the privileged. The Daytona Beach hospital, during wartime (WWII), located as it was next to a Naval Base for wounded seamen, was too full of bloody sailors on Bobby's birthday to accommodate Momma. So, he was born on the beachside, like a true Floridian.

During labor, Mother had an appendix attack, bringing Bobby out sooner than expected. He weighed only 4 pounds and 4 ounces. He's since turned out to be pretty healthy. Our beginnings aren't always good predictors of our futures.

We were in Athens in 1959, celebrating Christmas, when Daddy got the call saying that someone was going to buy the dairy. He rarely discusses business with us kids. We knew a little about it, but we didn't know the details. Daddy was always pretty closed-mouth about things until he did them.

In our first agricultural venture in Oconee County, Bobby wound up killing half of our chickens. It was poultry mass murder. He was innocently clipping their wings (you don't want them to fly off the farm) and then tossing the newly-flightless birds into a feed bin. He was moving at a good clip when he finally looked down into the bin and realized that he'd inadvertently suffocated the chickens at the bottom of the trough, killing about half of them.

Kay almost accidentally invented the underwater car. She tried to drown three cars in one day (which might have been a Daytona record). One weekend, when she was in college, Kay brought some girlfriends home with her. They wanted to see the beach, and, since you could drive right up to the shore, Kay, showing off a little for her wide-eyed Swedish friend, pulled too far onto the red, soft sand, too close to the shoreline and forgot entirely about how tides work. The tide came in and their car started to sink. They tried to rev it in reverse. It wasn't budging. That's when the dominoes started falling. Not wanting our parents to find about this, Kay tried to enlist the help of her brothers. They tried to hook her rapidly sinking automobile to the truck and pull it out that way. It didn't work. They tried again. Soon, both Kay's car and the brothers' "tow truck" began to sink. The water level was rising. All of the siblings were getting scared. Soon, the tide moved in far enough that the floorboard of her initial sunken car was about to float away to Davy Jones' Watery Junkyard. Having run out of options, they finally broke down and called the wrecker, who did manage to tow the car and the truck out of the sand before the ocean claimed them as its own. And yes, our parents found out.

After one of Billy's many, many injuries (the one that required a full-body cast, and yes, the one with the screw worms), we were all in the North Carolina mountain house when Billy's pain and itching became so bad that everyone knew that our vacation had ended. Being IN the full-body cast was torture for Billy, but on the trip back down to Florida, the rancid smell of the worms and Billy's own body odor, unwashed for months as he'd been, began to torture the rest of the family. Kay remembers vividly the smell being so powerfully bad that they had to roll all the windows down and stick their heads out the windows just to keep from throwing up. That whole episode, funny to reminisce about now, was simply gruesome.

EPILOGUE

Almost six decades have passed since Mama and Daddy put into practice their dream of moving back to Georgia and establishing a cattle farm. Though this dream came to life and then faded for them, the torch was passed to us, to our generation. We believe that we have been faithful to their vision, that we've kept the flame alive. Have we been "good and faithful servants"? YES!

The majority of the acreage of the Farm is still being used for cattle. Although small tracts of the property have been parceled and put to other land uses, which we've outlined in the story, we siblings feel as if Mama and Daddy would approve, as these uses, which would seem strange to them, still cling to the original family mission. The subdivision (Killarney West), the recreational complex, the college campus, the 4-lane federal highway, and the bank have all benefited the community, enhancing the lives of those locals who have made use of this new incarnation of "stewardship." The highest and best use of the land, the common good, the betterment of mankind, are all represented in these parcels.

We have played our part in the ever-unfolding drama of our family, adjusting with the times, but never bending core Bishop family principles.

Now, a new era for our family is dawning. This period will include development, an expanded college campus and the expansion of Highway 53. We are sounding the trumpets for the next generation to take up the torch, to keep it lit, to play their part in the family mission, and to carry the Bishop legacy into the future with the same sense of pride, humility, faith, and generosity we were taught by our parents.

A DISCLAIMER & A DEDICATION

This Bishop family history has been a labor of love, a true group effort. If, in the process of reading the book, you discover that the tone changes, that it feels like a different voice is guiding the current chapter compared to the previous chapter, that's because it is. We three all had a hand in the creation of the book. Though we all grew up under the same roof, with the same morals, the same relatives, and the same work ethics, we all saw things differently at times.

It makes sense when you think about it. We're the ones who lived these three distinctly different, but intimately interwoven, lives.

We three Bishop siblings would like to dedicate this book

to our dearly departed brother, Radford, always willing to share his gifts and possessions with his family.

Treasures

His greatest treasures
Were tattered and torn
The love letters he saved
Yellowed and worn.

The treasures he leaves me
Still so fresh and new
A bear hug and a smile
A compliment or two.

He'd tell me a story
I would tuck it away
A treasure to pull out
When I have a bad day.

I still can hear him say
Words that were his treasures
Family, friends, heritage
These were to him what mattered.

If you listen carefully

You are sure to hear
The words of his soul
Loud and clear.

His treasures now
Are greater than we can imagine
He's watching over us all
From his new home in heaven.

---poem by Meredith Bishop Marlowe, about her grandfather
Harrell Bishop

Kay---So, is that everything?

Bobby---I hope so. It ain't easy writing a book. Takes longer than I thought. It's important though.

Billy---Even more important now than when it was all happening.

Kay---We've had good lives. I'm not saying it's all been perfect. We've had our challenges, our share of tragedy. Lord knows, we all miss Radford. Still, on the whole, they've been good lives.

Bobby---Thanks to God's grace and our parents' values. You know, somehow I think our story would still be pretty much the same if Daddy had gone to school and gotten a degree and sold insurance or something.

Billy---Well, I don't know, Bobby. Can you seriously picture Daddy selling insurance?

Bobby---He still would've made us straighten out all those nails.

Billy---And gather all those cow patties.

Kay---We wouldn't have had cow patties if Daddy had been an insurance salesman, Billy.

Billy---I don't know. It's Daddy. Somehow he'd have found a way.

J.R. Charles

Johns Hopkins University

Stephen Shepard's Graduation
Medical College of Georgia

Scott Bishop – Studies Abroad London

Kerry Shepard

Western Carolina University

Robert Wesley Bishop

Piedmont College

Lauren Bishop

Oglethorpe University

Jonathan Luke Bishop

Georgia Southern University

Meredith's College Graduation

University of Georgia

Family Picture - Florida - 1998

Grandmother's 85th Birthday

Granddaddy with Sons and Grandsons

Christmas

Christmas with Grandchildren

Christmas Cruise

Thanksgiving

Thanksgiving 2003

Truett McConnell Dedication

Gene, Connor and pet cow

Summerlin-West 1938 - Family - Ridgewood Hotel

Harrell Bishop - Back Row - First on Left

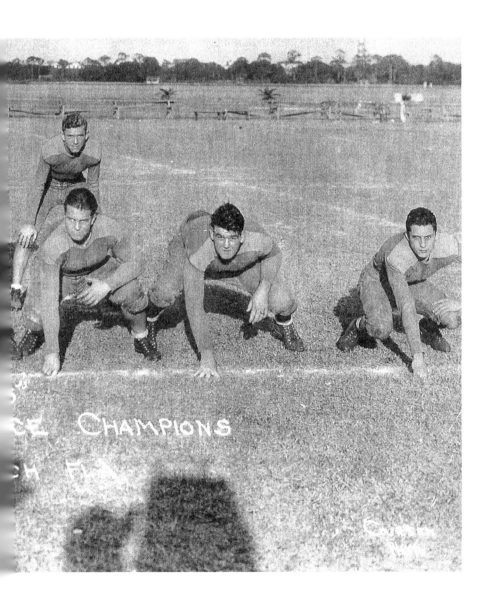

CPSIA information can be obtained
at www.ICGtesting.com
Printed in the USA
LVHW08s2023111018
593287LV00005B/20/P